The Grail

The Grail

A year ambling & shambling through an
Oregon vineyard in pursuit of the best pinot noir
wine in the whole wild world

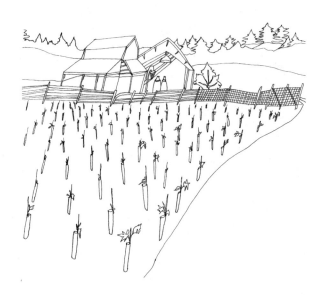

by

BRIAN DOYLE

drawings by

MARY MILLER DOYLE

OREGON STATE UNIVERSITY PRESS
Corvallis

The paper in this book meets the guidelines for permanence and durability of the Committee on Production Guidelines for Book Longevity of the Council on Library Resources and the minimum requirements of the American National Standard for Permanence of Paper for Printed Library Materials Z39.48-1984.

Library of Congress Cataloging-in-Publication Data

Doyle, Brian, 1956 Nov. 6—
The grail: a year ambling & shambling through an Oregon vineyard in pursuit of the best pinot noir wine in the whole wild world / by Brian Doyle; illustrations by Mary Miller Doyle.
  p. cm.
  ISBN-13: 978-0-87071-093-3 (alk. paper)
  ISBN-10: 0-87071-093-1 (alk. paper)
  1. Pinot noir (Wine)—Oregon.   2. Wine and wine making—Oregon.   I. Title.
TP557.D69 2006
641.2'2309795—dc22

2005032425

Text design by Jennifer Viviano.
Cover design by David Drummond.

OREGON STATE UNIVERSITY PRESS
500 Kerr Administration
Corvallis OR 97331-2122
541-737-3166 • fax 541-737-3170
http://oregonstate.edu/dept/press

For Jesse and Don Lange,
with grinning thanks for their many generosities;
and for my friend Gerald Asher, the best wine
writer there absolutely is, who taught me that writing
about wine is boring, but writing about people
is endlessly fascinating.

CONTENTS

The Grail

MAYBE PERHAPS MAYHAPS

A GLORIOUS GLEAMING GLITTERING October afternoon
in the red clay hills of Dundee, Oregon, where hawks
float by with writhing snakes in their beaks, and the deer
fences are eight feet high and lined with barbed wire to keep
out what grape growers call vineyard rats, and the BirdGard
machine in the middle of the vineyard is squawking the
warning cries of injured starlings at fifty decibels from four
speakers covering fifteen acres, and a thousand wasps are
having the most intoxicating day of their whole lives, and the
chief winemaker, the songwriter Don Lange, is cursing at the
moles and gophers that have riddled the dirt between the rows
of his vines, and musing about how maybe roasted gopher
would go *real* good with the wine from his vineyard, and
twenty people sweating like mad are picking grapes faster
than you have ever seen anyone pick grapes before in your
whole life, and the intense younger winemaker, Don's son

Jesse, is driving a careening forklift truck at twenty miles an hour up and down the alleys between the rows, picking up bins the pickers have filled from the ends of the rows, and the operations manager, Wally, is cursing quietly but thoroughly as he tries to fix a fermenting tank, and the sales manager, Laura, is not selling or managing anything at all but instead picking madly through the dump tray for mangled grapes and wasps as a river of grapes and leaves and stems and wasps rockets by her on the way to the crushing machine, and the cellarmaster, Chuy, is sluicing juice out of the crushing machine and delivering it right quick into the fermenter or the press, which is to say red wine or white wine, which makes a huge difference here in the red hills of Dundee, because while the juice in the press will make excellent chardonnay and pinot gris and riesling and pinot blanc, the juice in the fermenters will make maybe perhaps mayhaps the Best Pinot Noir Wine in the World, which is a remarkable thing to say about wine from soil that is adamantly not French, and exactly the reason why everyone is working so madly this afternoon, because this is Harvest, the World Series and Super Bowl and World Cup and Grand Final of winemaking, and if the Holy Grail is to be found, which is what pinot noir winemakers call the Best Pinot Noir Wine in the World, it begins here, this week, on this gleaming hill, in the crisp brilliant sun, with the Cascade Mountains glittering snowily to the east and the Coast Range mountains rolling greenly to the west, with a hundred tons of purple-black grapes the size of fingernails roaring by like a murky dusty river, and Wally cursing like a drunken sailor.

GLEE IN THE GLASS

A FEW YEARS AGO a friend of mine briefly lost her mind financially and bought a whole case of Lange wine, which is terrific wine but by no means cheap. She stopped at the winery on her way to the Oregon coast, and something about the winery and vineyard waaay up there on its beaming hill absorbed her, and once up there she found the chief winemaker and his winemaking son to be dry-witted and friendly, and lawd the wine was fine, and there was a lot to be said, as she said, for sitting high on a hill on a brilliant afternoon with a glass of pinot in your paw, so while she was just going to buy a bottle or two as her contribution to a salmon dinner at the coast that night she ended up, what the hell, life's short, buying a whole case.

In one sense this was no surprise, because she is crazy generous and deeply fond of the grand gesture, but in another sense it was startling, because generally she has about eleven cents on hand and she ransacks the cushions of her car for change and she once spent a year eating nothing but potatoes and she spent another year when young and unfiltered collecting food from the forest and selling what she did not eat from a ratty roadside stand in a town where it rains more than a hundred inches a year. Which is another whole story, part of which has to do with her collecting psychedelic mushrooms in the rain from muddy boggy meadows while huge dripping cows watched disinterestedly and vast bulls pondered whether or not to rev up their thousand pounds of angry meat and destroy the sprinting giggling intruder.

Anyway the two bottles she opened that night were my first bottles of Lange—pinot gris and chardonnay, as I recall, for at that time I was young and raw and drank only white wines, not yet comprehending the complex characters and allures of reds, the muscle of merlot, the sunshine of shiraz, the nuance of nebbiolo, the burl and brawn of brunello and barbaresco, the hurrah of syrah, the poetry of pinot noir. I spake as a child, I understood as a child, I drank the wines of a child, largely because the first wines I ever tasted as a callow teenager had once been apples and berries and motor oil and such.

But then my wife, who likes expeditions, led an expedition to the Lange vineyard and winery way up there on its beaming hill, and something about the vineyard and the winery and the cheerfulness of the winemaker and his astute amiable son absorbed me too, and lawd the wine was fine, and so my wife and I took to stopping by the winery occasionally, and basking and blinking in the sun like lounging lizards, and shooting the breeze with Don and Jesse, who were indeed dry-witted and friendly, and the thought occurred to me, while sipping, that sipping this particular wine on this particular hill with the men who made it from this very dirt was pretty cool, and that someone young and footloose and energetic really ought to try to catch some of the riveting story of how these two men turn acres of tiny black grapes into terrific complex wine every year.

I mean, how actually is wine *made*? For all that so many of us drink wine and buy wine and read about wine and make gifts of wine to each other and visit wineries and vineyards and see movies about wine and talk pseudoknowledgeably about wine, very few of us, it seems to me, have the faintest notion of how grapes get to be glee in the glass. I have savored many wines over the years, and enjoyed not only taste and tipsiness but the way good wine adds ceremony and memory and joy and sometimes sacramentality to meals and moments, but the actual creation and manufacture and science of the stuff is a total mystery to me. Wines to me are like cars and computers and children and women, among which fleets and flocks I swim daily and understand, technically, zero.

You could write it as a series of little friendly stories, really, I said to Jesse one brilliant October day not long after harvest, as we drank the first bottlings of the previous year's harvest at the Langes' annual post-harvest party. It wouldn't be that hard. You'd just have to wander up here regularly and ask questions.

Makes sense to me, said Jesse, pouring me another dollop of his pinot noir.

Plus, you know, it's really interesting that you guys are, by your own account, completely devoted to making unbelievable pinot noir that maybe, all things considered, might be among the best pinot noir in the world. That's nuts. That's crazy ambitious.

Hmm, said Jesse.

You could write a story like that over the course of a year, I said, warming to my great idea for somebody else to do. You could do it from harvest to harvest maybe, and that way give a sense of what it's really *like* to grow and make wine and to chase after a truly great wine. I mean, not the usual huffy snuffy nonsense about bouquet and ambiance and nose and *can be cellared up to ten thousand years* in tiny arrogant sniffy type on the label, but the real *work* of wine, you know, the sheer *labor* of it, the creativity, the dust, the bugs, the machinery, the botany, the chemistry, the wild nuttiness of trying to make a great wine, the redness of the dirt, the entrepreneurialishness of the thing, the way big hawks loom over the vineyard like grumpy airplanes, the whole burrito, you know what I mean?

And the slipperiness of evil distributors, said Jesse.

Yeh, that too, I said. Man, this wine is remarkable.

And clients who never actually *pay* their bills, said Jesse.

Yeh, I said. Listen, you're fixating, and this wine is superb.

We did okay with this, said Jesse, who is very polite.

Okay? *Okay* is as far as you'll go?

Great grapes, said Jesse, smiling. Winemakers who knew how to get out of the way of great grapes.

See, even that, I said, that sort of remark, that's how winemakers think, right?

Well . . . some do.

And see, it's cool that the wine in my glass was born right here, I say, even if this wine is swill. Which dirt exactly did this terrible wine come from?

The old pinot block, says Jesse, c'mon, I'll show you, and we take our glasses and amble downhill into a thicket of pinot noir vines taller than our heads, their leaves just beginning to go golden and scarlet and orange, and Jesse starts talking, in his eager fascinated confident cheerful cautious informed erudite friendly way, and so begins this story.

WINE-ENTHUSIASTIC &
WINE-SPECTATORIAL

F OR A WHILE I took sheaves and reams and gobs and
slabs of notes, pretty much scribbling like a madman
every time Jesse opened his mouth, and reading tomes about
winemaking and viniculture and viticulture and oenology, and
lurching and skidding haphazardly through the vast mad
maze of the World Wide Wild Web, and quizzing wine
stewards and wine shopkeepers and wine geeks and wine
aficionados, and brazenly stealing wine-enthusiastic and wine-
spectatorial magazines from doctors' and dentists' offices, and
flipping through glossy gleamy shiny francotitled magazines
the size of halibut, and soon I found myself dazed and
confused amid facts and details and numbers and phrases,
very little of which spoke to me in any language that I
personally knew, so finally I conceded something which I have
lately conceded a lot, which is that I really only understand
little stories, my brain only sparks to life when little stories are
fed into it like berries into babies, so one day I said to Jesse,
Hey, do me a favor, just tell me little stories, lay out the whole
year for me in about five minutes, a sketch of what really
happens, a year in the life of the vineyard?

Hmm, okay, well, it's November now, said Jesse, and the
harvest is all in, the new pinot noir is all in barrel, the new
white wines are in tanks or barrels, all the equipment is shiny
and clean, so where are we right now? We're screwed. We are
woefully behind with the things we didn't do for the last
month because we were harvesting the grapes and making the
wines, which things are repair, maintenance, inventory, bottling,

labeling, sales, distribution, marketing, and a thousand other things I can't remember at the moment. The first thing to remember about making wine is that you hardly ever get to make wine, and the second thing to remember is that you always have waaay more to do than actually making wine.

Sounds like fun, I said.

Hmm.

And what's happening in the vineyard?

Gearing down for the winter, he said. The vines are deciduous, of course, so they lose chlorophyll, shut down systems, close up shop, go dormant. There's a flare of color and then they lose their leaves and basically they hibernate, although this is when there's major root growth, an inch a day, because their energy heads down now, not up. So November December January, we basically let them sleep. They've worked hard and now they are entitled to zone out. We give them a little nutrient spray and put them to bed and essentially turn the vineyard off. We might put down some grass seed to fend off erosion from the winter rains. Then in February we prune, to shape the vines for the growing season; March is bud break, which basically means the vines wake up; April and May they grow like crazy; they bloom in June, which means the vines pop their flowers, and there's a week or so there when there's the coolest smell in the world, the scent of grape flowers, which are these little infinitesimally tiny stars, so little you can hardly see them, but if the breeze is right you catch an amazing scent, and we have more than twenty thousand vines here, so make a point to be here in June, but sometimes the scent lasts like only an hour, so don't miss it.

Okay.

I'm serious.

Okay.

So during flowering, he continues, the vines are fertilizing themselves and each other, because they are hermaphroditic, and then ninety days from bloom to harvest is the general rule of thumb.

How do you know the right moment for harvest? I ask, trying to stay focused on the matter at hand and not think about the wild seething scene in the vineyard, the vines fertilizing each other madly when no one is looking, the little tiny bras, the little tiny cigarettes, the recriminations at dawn.

Well, there are about ninety factors to that decision too, he says, grinning. There's sugar levels in the grapes, color, weather, crew schedules, delivery schedules from other vineyards. But the foremost factor is my dad. He decides. We walk through the vineyard a lot in the last few days before harvest, testing and tasting. And as he says there's a certain scent on the hill once the grapes are just right for picking.

Have you smelled it?

Some, he says. I've only done seven harvests here, and one in New Zealand. But he's done more than twenty, and to be honest, for all the science, and testing brix, which is sugar levels, and analyzing water retention in the grape, and charting weather patterns, and watching the birds, who have a sixth sense about when the grapes are just right for stealing from us, a lot of knowing when to harvest and a lot of making wine is experience and intuition and feel, which is pretty cool. Making wine is *not* an art, I don't like that sort of talk, but it most certainly *is* a craft, and some people are masters at it. Especially here. There are a lot of terrific winemakers in this valley.

Like who? I ask. Who are the great winemakers in the valley?

Hmm, he says. I like everybody.

C'mon, I say, tell me, who's the competition? I mean, whose wines do you rank with yours?

I like everybody, he says, smiling.

I name a pinot noir from the valley that I myself have personally tasted and found to be overpriced underdone swill, and then I name a pinot from a vineyard less than a mile away that is an amazing and terrific wine but you have to take out a second mortgage to buy a bottle and the winery is owned by one of those acronymic corporations you've never heard of that turns out to own half the planets in the solar system, and I pose these two wines as alpha and omega on a scale of comparative quality and bang for the buck, and inquire as to where along that scale one might find the various pinot noirs made right here on this hill by the Langes père and fils, but Jesse won't take the bait, although he does finally say, still smiling, that one thing I should remember about the valley is that it is, all things considered, a fairly small valley, where everyone

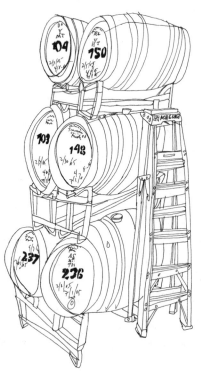

knows each other, and untoward and hubristic remarks circulate fast, and he actually personally himself lives in the valley, and I do not, and I see what he's getting at, so we shift gears back to winemaking.

Do you do anything special to prepare for harvest? I ask.

Yep, says Jesse. You prepare for it like you would prepare for a football game or something. You eat more and sleep more in the weeks leading up to harvest. Harvest is *intense*. It's exhausting. Tempers flare. You're going from four in the morning until midnight, as a rule, and everything *has* to run perfectly, there's no time or patience for mistakes or fooling around or visitors. People always want to come up and help with the harvest, they have this romantic bucolic idea of it, and we politely tell them nope, no way. You're in the vineyard at dawn and you work your ass off all day and you're cleaning equipment every night until the place is spotless. You hardly have time to eat, let alone sleep. You lose weight and people get testy. But harvest has a narrative arc to it, sort of—there's a moment when you sense that it's *happened*, the bulk of the work is done, you're over the hump. *That's* a great moment. Everyone working harvest senses that at about the same time, and often that moment is celebrated that night with a great dinner. Like last year we sat around on hump night, the whole crew, and had a long relaxed late dinner that went waaaay past midnight. Beautiful clear warm night too. Lots of beer. It was hard to clean the equipment *that* night, I'll tell you. That's a great feeling, though. I mean, there's still work to be done, fruit to bring in, wine to be made, but you're over the hill, you can relax a little, you've actually done what really is the whole point of the operation—getting the grapes in. There's a huge sense of relief and accomplishment. Which lasts about ten minutes, until you realize how screamingly behind you are in every other aspect of the operation. Which is pretty much the situation every other day of the year. Including today. So let's get hopping, he concludes, and we walk back up to the winery, through the curling golden leaves of the slumbering vines.

THE GOOD OLD DAYS

T HE ROOTS OF THE pinot noir vine are lost in antiquity. Italian winemakers will tell you that the warrior Aedui people brought it to Burgundy from their invasions of Italy, or that the Roman Empire brought it, as the vine they called *Helvenacia minor*, to Burgundy when Rome conquered Gaul. French winemakers will tell you that the rootstock grew wild in Burgundy before any imperial Italian trooper ever set foot in Gaul, and that the wild vine was cultivated by the native tribes into a vine called *Vitis allobergica*, from which they made a wine famous since the first century after Christ. Unlike their Roman masters, who stored wine in clay jars, the Gallic peoples of Burgundy stored their wine in wooden casks, usually oak. Wars and empires swirled through Gaul as the centuries whirled by but the making of wine from *Vitis allobergica* changed not; season after season for two thousand years the grapes called pinot (pine cone, for the shape of the cluster) were gathered, crushed, fermented, casked, and eventually sipped with ceremony and merriment, or merrimony and cerement, depending on how much wine was sipped. And with ritual prayer; no wine was more popular in medieval France as the miraculous liquid of the Catholic Mass, the elixir that mysteriously and magically is transformed during the ceremony into the actual blood of the Christ to be absorbed into the bloodstreams of the faithful, and thousands of casks of excellent pinot noir were annually shipped to the Pope, sometimes as payment of levies, as the Holy Roman Catholic Church essentially owned Burgundy until the French Revolution in 1789.

The Good Old Days, as Catholic friends of mine say sighing.

The largest plantings of pinot noir are still in France, mostly in the Côte d'Or, the famous Slope of Gold, a strip of Burgundy about two miles wide and thirty miles long with chalky soils and quick drainage and an angle of repose that makes painters swoon, but the fruit called the poet's grape hit the road in the twentieth century—both to countries with ancient or modern wine cultures and industries (Greece, Germany, Austria, Italy, Australia, New Zealand, Argentina, South Africa) and to nations not often mentioned on wine lists (Algeria, Brazil, China, Canada, Japan, Bulgaria, Serbia, Macedonia, Mexico), and even to many states not often mentioned on wine lists (Ohio, Colorado, Texas, Utah, Arizona, New Mexico).

It wears many names around the world. In Austria, pinot noir is called Blauburgunder. In Germany it is called Spätburgunder. In Switzerland it is called Clevner. In Yugoslavia it is called Burgundac. In Italy it is called, delightfully, Pinot Nero. In Australia a winemaker friend of mine calls it Peanut Waah and says that it is a haunted siren of a grape, a femme fatale, a grape you are fatally drawn to and which will drag you to your doom, which is whoiy, he says in his smiling sunny slanguage, it's called Waah, because it will make you wail and gnash your teeth and wonder under what dark star you were born to be so bedeviled and accursed.

Pinot noir arrived in America sometime around the California gold rush of 1848, perhaps imported as cuttings by a Frenchman named Pierre Pellier, or perhaps via the colorful charlatan Colonel Agoston Haraszthy de Mokcsa, or perhaps via the Frenchman Charles Lefranc, no one knows, but by the 1880s it was being grown in the Napa, Sonoma, and Livermore valleys (and on Santa Cruz Island, off Santa Barbara), and small plots and bottlings of pinot noir survived both the phylloxera epidemic of the 1880s (a plague of insects) and the Prohibition epidemic of 1920–1933 (a plague of teetotallers).

By 1941 American pinot noir, wrote the wine scholar and importer and merchant Frank Schoonmaker, "is beginning to yield, under favorable conditions, as good wines as it yields in general in France."

Yet it remained essentially a cult wine, almost a hobby for winemakers, a sidelong sideways glance, a quiet obscure cousin of the rising king of California, cabernet sauvignon; and even as pinot plantings spread (to the Alexander and Russian River valleys, to San Benito County, and especially to the foggy Carneros district of Napa), pinot production remained small and hullabaloo and hoopla smaller.

Then came 1966, a remarkable year altogether: a Jewish child was born in Spain for the first time in 374 years, Ronald Reagan was elected boss of California, Indira Gandhi was elected boss of India, the Soviets landed a Luna spacecraft on the moon, John Lennon opined dryly that the Beatles were more popular than Jesus, Haile Selassie visited Jamaica, the Grateful Dead moved to a house on Haight Street, the Americans landed a Surveyor spacecraft on the moon, Montgomery Clift died, the Beatles released *Revolver*, "Star Trek" was first televised, Namibia declared independence, Jimmy Hendrix changed his name to Jimi, LSD was declared illegal, Catholics began to eat meat on Fridays, Barbados declared independence, the Americans bombed Hanoi, Walt Disney died, Kwanzaa was invented, Tom Stoppard wrote *Rosencrantz and Guildenstern Are Dead*, Arlo Guthrie wrote "Alice's Restaurant," Hewlett-Packard introduced its first computer, Buster Keaton died, Guyana declared independence, Malaysia and Indonesia declared peace, taekwando was invented, Lesotho declared independence, Thich Nhat Hanh visited America, Bill Evans opened a long run at the Village Vanguard jazz club, and a young guy named David Lett, the son of a Utah farmer, finished his undergraduate education, contemplated the meager professional prospects of his philosophy degree, decided to go on to dental school, detoured through the Napa Valley on the way to dental school, totally lost his desire to be a dentist, and soon thereafter, against all enological advice, planted pinot noir cuttings in the Red Hills of Dundee. So began Eyrie Vineyards, named for a hawk nest nearby, and so began Oregon pinot noir, the first bottle of which sold for $2.65 (as "Oregon spring wine"), which soon thereafter led to Don Lange buying a hillside covered with raspberry canes.

Today there are many thousands of acres of pinot noir planted in California, but the Golden State is not thought to be the home of pinot noir wine good enough to challenge the Burgundians for the world title: Oregon is. And in Oregon the best pinot noir is grown and made in and around the Red Hills of Dundee, an area now renowned enough for its wines to be the first in Oregon to be granted its own appellation—wine talk for regional identity strong enough to be so noted on the bottle, as a marketing gig.

Six of the twenty-five biggest producers of wine in Oregon are in Dundee. Six more are near Dundee and share the same fast-draining volcanic soils that help make the Yamhill Valley perfect for growing pinot noir. The other thirteen of the largest wineries are in the Eola Hills, in the central Willamette Valley; in the Umpqua Valley in the southwest corner of the state, near the Siskyou Mountains; or in the gentle hills just west of the city of Portland. (One, the McMenamin Edgefield Winery, is actually *in* the city, on the grounds of what was once the metropolitan poor farm.)

Lange Winery is not one of the twenty-five biggest wineries, and has no particular plans to be.

We made a little over eleven thousand cases of wine this year, says Jesse, which is a long way from our first bottling, which was nine hundred cases, in 1987. We might make twelve thousand cases next year, I guess, and maybe five or ten years down the road, after we get the rest of the property planted and fruiting, we might top out at fifteen thousand cases. But I don't see it in the near future. We make enough wine and we basically make enough money. I mean, it would be great to make more money, we have a lot of debts to pay off, but I like that we make great wine and a lot of people can afford it. I like it that we have a very fine pinot noir that you don't have to be rich to buy. I like that we are not a cult wine. I like that it's not just wine geeks who know us and drink our wine and come to the winery. I like it that people come up here to taste the wines and have picnics and meet us. We could sell a lot more wine if we *made* a lot more wine but then we would be in sales all the time and not making wine and talking to the people who like our wine.

I like the tasting room, he continues. I worked there for two years and I still help out on weekends. We get good people there, partly because you have to make an effort to get up here to the winery. And things happen up here you can't anticipate or measure. Like last weekend a couple was here, the guy asked the woman to marry him in the morning, and she said yes, and to celebrate they came up here, and we got to talking, and I found out they were headed back into the city that night but didn't have dinner reservations. I called the wine steward at a restaurant I know and reserved them a table and arranged for great champagne, and, you know, they were thrilled. Look, here's the note they sent me yesterday. Isn't that cool? Lange means something to them more than the wine. Which is pretty cool. You can't measure that. That kind of thing happens all the time.

Why champagne? I ask. Why not a bottle of Lange on the table?

Because I am not a total sales geek, he says. You don't mess with a champagne moment.

CHEERFUL HEADLONG WALLY TALK

DECEMBER. I WANDER UP to the vineyard and spend the afternoon walking the perimeter with Wally. This takes a long time, partly because fifteen acres is a serious number of acres when you are circumferencing rather than diagonalling, and partly because Wally is a world-class talker, one of those force-of-nature creatures who are absolutely fascinated in and by everything, and funny and passionate and erudite and energetic and can walk and talk all day, which it seems to me after a while we are certainly going to do.

I ask him a single question: *tell me about the natural history of the vineyard, you know, the animals and birds and plants and insects and funguses and all?,* and his eyes light up behind his spectacles and he starts talking and I start scribbling while we are both walking downhill so that my notes are all written with a downhill slant that makes me grin every time I see it because it reminds me of cheerfulheadlongwallytalk which, approximated, was something like:

Waalllllll, you have your occasional raccoon and coyote and fox, and badgers and porcupines, and rabbits, we have little rabbits and big rabbits, the cottontails and jacks, and then newts, toads, and tree frogs, which some people call peepers or chorus frogs because when they sing all together at night that's an amazing sound, and we have turtles and skinks, which are quick skinny lizards impossible to catch, and boa snakes and racer snakes and gopher snakes, which are big and hungry enough to eat rabbits, and garter snakes, which people also call garden snakes or sometimes gartysnakes, and possums and shrews and moles and ground squirrels, which are big things cousin to marmots and woodchucks, you know, and also gray

squirrels and Doug squirrels, which we call chickarees, and
mice and moles and voles and gophers, and right here we have
an endemic species, you know, the camas gopher, which lives
only in this one valley in the whole world, which is pretty neat,
although it will eat the roots of the vines if given a chance,
which we don't, and there's bats, and then there are the birds,
of which there are probably a hundred kinds, I'll just rattle off
the first ones that come to my mind, there's your herons, which
float over the vineyard sometimes, a grand sight, and geese, and
you might see a sandhill crane here and there, and there's all
sorts of ducks, and vultures and osprey, and eagles and hawks,
there's several kinds of hawks, redtails and sharpshins and
cooperhawks and kestrels, which some people call
sparrowhawks, and pheasants, and grouse, and quail, those are
the little California quail, the ones you see running alongside
the road in little chain gangs, and there's killdeer, and pigeons
of course, and doves, and all sorts of owls, you have your
barnies and hornies and screech-owls, and nighthawks and
swifts, and hummingbirds and woodpeckers, and here and
there you see a lark but not as many as there used to be, and
there's swallows, of course, and jays, there's the Steller's jay and
the scrub jay and they don't like each other much, and crows
and ravens and chickadees, and nuthatches and wrens, and
dippers in the creeks hereabouts, which they used to be called
ouzels, lovely word, and then there's the dark side, the enemy:
robins, starlings, waxwings, those are the worst, they come
down on the grapes in flocks, and there's all sorts of warblers in
season, of course, and towhees in the brush, and your various
sparrows, of which the most beautiful singer is probably your
white-crowned sparrow even more so than the song sparrow, *I*
think so anyway, and then there's your juncos and blackbirds,
and finches, and occasionally an oriole. That's all the birds I
can think of at the moment. But then there's your bigger
animals, well, there's muskrat and beaver in the valley, but not

here, we're too high up on the hill, though there's a little creek
down by the fence, but I haven't seen beaver here, and you
would know if there were beaver around, it's not like they're shy
about what they're doing, and there's weasel and mink and
otter around the creeks, and there's bobcats sometimes you see
them, and a lot of skunk hereabouts. Bears and lions, no, not
here, there's not enough wild land, but there's lion and bear in
the hills there to the west where the real forest begins and goes
all the way to the coast, which is where you'll find elk also.
Badger, fisher, lynx, no, no, they'd all be over on the other side
of the mountains to the east there, the Cascades, or down
south in the Siskiyou Mountains. Biggest animal we've had in
the vineyard is the vineyard rat, which can get to be three
hundred pounds, you know, which is a serious size animal,
especially with an animal that can hop that fence.

The vineyard rat?

Our bitter enemy, says Wally. The scourge of vineyards
everywhere. That's why we built the fence, which was one of
the labors of Hercules, I'll tell you. Jesse and I built that fence
and it took us one solid month and I hope never to build a
fence like that as long as I live, which won't be long if I ever
have to build another fence like that.

THE ENEMY

THE VINEYARD RAT WEIGHS upwards of three hundred pounds and is nearly four feet tall at the shoulder. It can sprint forty miles an hour, soar more than twenty feet in a single bound, and easily clear an eight-foot fence. It can live comfortably in a forest soaked by two hundred inches of rain a year. It can live in a desert spattered by four inches of rain a year. It has been found living on mountains that have ice and snow all year long. It has been found in prairie grasslands. It lives in the Yukon and it lives in the Yucatan. It has been found in elementary school playgrounds and library gardens and cemeteries and churchyards and airport runways and football fields and tree farms and cornfields and anywhere else it can find the fresh green plant buds it loves, and the fresh green buds it loves best of all are those on grapevines, which is why the blacktailed deer, *Odocoileus hemionus columbianus*, is called the vineyard rat, and why when Wally and Jesse built a fence around the vineyard, by hand, with labor they shiver to remember, they lined the top of the fence with barbed wire— *to castrate all the males if possible*, says Wally darkly.

But the vineyard rat, with a leaping ability that would make Michael Jordan gape, is not the only enemy of vine and vineyard and winery and glowering winemaker. No: there are the possum and the raccoon, who love grapes, and the coyote, who occasionally cops a cluster, and the rabbit, who loooves to eat young vines, and the hawk moth, whose larvae looove grape leaves, and mealybugs and curculios and aphids and beetles and termites and cutworms and lo their many insectavoracious cousins who love to eat of the vine and the fruit of the vine, most notably and legendarily the dreaded phylloxera, a tiny yellow insect that gobbles the roots and leaves of grapevines, but there are also funguses and diseases like mildew and botrytis and leafroll and fanleaf, and vast armies of birds, especially robins and starlings and jays and thrushes, not to mention blackbirds, waxwings, crows, woodpeckers, pigeons, and even bats, all the winged things who swoop in to eat grapes seemingly hours before they are to be picked for the crush, and who are battled with, as the wine writer Philip Wagner once noted with relish, "firecrackers, acetylene cannon, phonograph records of their warning cry, stuffed owls hung in conspicuous places and intended to frighten, helicopters, balloons with mechanical noisemakers, rockets, plastic and metal whirligigs strung on cords, blank cartridges, arm-waving, popguns, gongs, dishpans, scarecrows, strips of tobacco cloth, expensive plastic cobwebs, and an infinity of other feeble defenses."

At Lange Winery, defense of the crop against air attack is entrusted to the BirdGard Electronic Bird Repeller, invented by the Bird-X company of Chicago, which also makes the BirdXpeller, the CritterBlaster Pro, the GooseBuster, the IrriTape (a pennant made of iridescent foil), the Prowler Owl (a plastic great horned owl nearly four feet wide, with patented flapping wings and a heart-stopping glare), the Terror-Eyes (a vinyl balloon owl face, with eyes that rotate in their sockets), the Bird-Lite (which emits million-candlepower red, white, and blue flashes), a slew of other anti-bird ointments and nets and gels, plastic alligator heads (to scare away wading birds), and powdered fox and coyote urine. Among other things. But it is the Repeller on which the Langes bet their crop every year, and they are *big* Repeller fans. Without the Repeller playing defense (at fifty decibels every two minutes during daylight hours from July through harvest in October), resident and migratory birds would eat maybe a ton of grapes every year, estimates Jesse—about a thousand bottles of some of the best pinot noir wine in the world.

So we *like* the machine, he says. Tell you the truth, you don't hear it after a while. Which means either that your brain processes the sound out of your consciousness or we are all deaf as doors.

Yet for all Jesse's leeriness of birds and the damage they can inflict, the greatest natural enemy of the vineyard, he says, is one you can hardly see, one that he worries about weekly, one he sees in his darkest dreams: the dreaded phylloxera, the infinitesimal yellow louse, the winemaker's nightmare. *Daktulosphaira vitifoliae*, entomologists call it, and winemakers know it well, for the tiny animal dearly loves to eat grapevines, and has killed many millions of acres of plants over the centuries. Its life is fascinating: an egg laid late autumn, and stashed under the bark of the trunk or cane of the vine, awakes at the first hint of spring [swelling music by Aaron Copland], at which point it squirms and thrashes and opens [aaaaiiiieeee] to reveal the Fundatrix, or Stem Mother [the brooding source of all evil, played by the late Anne Bancroft in heavy makeup], who searches for a fresh new succulent innocent shoot of the vine and begins to snarf it like a skinny deacon at a church buffet. The grapevine, horrified at being lunched upon, reacts by imprisoning the intruder in a tiny yellow cell under the new leaf. Inside this cell, called a gall, the Stem Mother grins horribly and her womb churns and she begins [eeeewwwww] to emit offspring, not two or ten but hundreds and hundreds! who crawl from the Fundatrixial gall and begin to feed on new shoots! which occasions more galls being formed by the reeling grapevine! even as some of the Stem Mother's sea of children are growing wings and becoming adults and emerging into the brilliant world and laying eggs all over the vine and the smaller eggs become males and the larger eggs become females and they mate [all the *mating* in a vineyard, who knew?] and in late autumn the female [Angelina Jolie, slumming a little] lays a single ominous egg under the bark of a cane or trunk [screen fades to black but clearly a sequel is in the works, wild speculation that Sigourney Weaver will replace Angelina Jolie, rumors of catfights on the set] . . .

Entomologists believe that phylloxera originally entered the universe in the eastern United States, spreading throughout America and prompting American grapevines to evolve their own resistance, in the ancient war of wits and weapons between predator and prey, plant and parasite. In 1863, however, the tiny louse went to Europe, probably carried on rootstock or vineyard equipment, and within a few years phylloxera had killed some 70 percent of France's grapevines, a stunning blow to a nation justifiably proud of its wine heritage and quality. In Burgundy, where the Best Pinot Noir in the World was made for centuries (and still is, insist the French), the louse killed more than half the vines that produced the poet's grape.

The French found two weapons that worked against phylloxera—flooding the vineyard, which drowned the insects, and spraying carbon bisulphide, which killed them outright. Both approaches were hard to accomplish, however, and soon the French realized, to their dismay, that the best and most thorough solution was the most culturally unthinkable one—to tear out the native vines and replant with American rootstock resistant to the louse. This they did, with immense Francowailing and gnashing of teeth and Gallic insult to the nation from which the yellow peril had come; but in one of the million savory ironies of the human story, the new vines, for many reasons, produced even better wine than before. Thus the American peril provoked the planting in France of American vines producing French wine generally better than American wine from American vines in America—except, maybe, perhaps, mayhaps, it may be, possibly, beginning in the late twentieth century, in the Red Hills of Dundee.

YAMHELAS

THERE ARE THREE THOUSAND people in and around the town of Dundee, which is pretty much half hills and half not. The vineyards are in the west hills and the farms are on the flat eastern fields. The town is divided by a highway and competing visions of its future. Once in a while an angry resident will post a sign on the outskirts of town decrying the (relatively) new wine industry, but the signs fade away after a while. The sign I remember best was an enormous cloth hung on a decrepit wooden cabin in the center of town. I don't remember the exact wording but I remember the prickly fury of the message and the words *elitist* and *property tax*. The cloth sagged there for months, getting grayer and shaggier, until somebody bought the cabin and removed the cloth and painted the shack purple and opened an espresso shop.

Dundee, which draws its name from the Scottish town of the same name, lies on the far east end of Yamhill County, which draws its name from the Yamhelas or Cheamhill people who lived here for perhaps eight thousand years before malaria and war and exile and commerce shoved them off the land and into history. The Yamhelas, according to anthropologists, enjoyed a stunning variety of wild foods in their temperate valley, among them elk, rabbit, deer, mushrooms, salmon, grouse, goose, duck, and trout—all foods that go particularly well with pinot noir. The Yamhelas were also renowned for their annual brush burns, which promoted the growth of, among many other plants, wild grapes. There is no record of the Yamhelas harvesting wild grapes and fermenting the juice and sitting around talking about bouquet and cellarability, but sometimes on sunny days in the valley I imagine a cheerful humming Yamhelas father and son making wine on Don and Jesse's hill and storing it in barrels they have carved from the mammoth local white oaks and opening the barrels a year later with extensive intricate religious ceremonies and conducting sprawling harvest parties that draw visitors from clans for miles around and leave most of the adult population roaring and singing amid the oaks and thickets of wild vines.

Yamhill County, created by white folks in 1843, was once immense, stretching from the Willamette River to the ocean and from the Columbia River to the California border, an acreage bigger than many eastern states, but time and politics whittled it down to normal county size, and today it is about seven hundred square miles, most of which is still farms, though there are now eighty wineries in the county and more than five thousand acres of vineyards.

And those five thousand acres will double in the next five years, you mark my words, says Don, although me, personally, I think most of the very best land for grapes is taken. That's certainly the case in these hills. I mean, there are some lots available, yes, for unbelievably high prices, ridiculous prices really, though someone *will* pay those prices, you mark my words. But the land that's *best* suited for pinot noir here, that's pretty much gone. I mean, people here aren't stupid. People have been growing grapes and making wine here for nearly forty years, and winemakers are serious students of the land, you know. We all know geology and water tables and retention rates and soils and drainage patterns and weather factors and microclimes and which pockets of which hills retain fog pockets, stuff like that. You *have* to know that. You wouldn't *buy* the land if you didn't understand it as thoroughly as you possibly could. And then, of course, after you plant your vines, everything you understand goes right out the window and it's up to the weather to cooperate in making the great grapes you need for great wine. So ultimately all winemakers are climatologists also. You develop a seventh sense for the weather. Which drives you crazy, because the thing you need the most for great wine, after great soil and great plants, is great weather, and of all the things in the universe that you haven't the slightest control over, it's the weather. So winemakers all go crazy in the end. That's a fact. Trust me. Every wine-growing region should have a central facility to house and care for all the winemakers who went off their nuts making wine there.

EXHILARATION & EXHALATION

JANUARY. I WANDER UP to the vineyard through a red dust so thick along the road that it coats the walls of blackberry bushes defining the vineyard. Flurries and scurries and hurries of quail in the bushes, a shivering goldfinch surfing a swaying thistle, a wind-riffled ground squirrel perched on a fencepost like a nervous fur hat, a wheeling hawk looking for a furry lunch.

Jesse and I wander through the old pinot noir block. This was the first block planted, sixteen years ago, and the stalks are as thick as wrists.

In season, says Jesse, there's a green confidence in this block, a certain . . . maturity of attitude, choosing his words carefully.

What, in the vines? I ask, looking at him closely; for such a young guy he has a dark quirky wit that has more than once made me snort with laughter.

Look, I'm no vine-hugger, he says. But, yeh, there is a certain form of communication, let's say, between the vines and the winemaker. Right after we harvest, you know, there's a sense of exhilaration and exhalation in the vineyard. We're thrilled that we're done and everything in and safe and all the hard labor is finished, but also the vines are satisfied, you know? You can feel it. They exist to produce grapes, and they have done so brilliantly, and we have taken their fruit, and so communicated to them that their job is done, now they can rest, and you're grinning at me, but I am not kidding, we'll walk through the blocks after harvest and you can almost hear them sigh with relief as they get ready to go dormant.

So pruning in winter is a wake-up call? I ask.

Yeh, in a sense, says Jesse. You are indicating to the vines that it's time to prepare for the impending season. People forget that a vine is a living creature with an acute sensory apparatus. And the most sensitive and touchy and weird of all grapevines is pinot noir. Which is why winemakers call it the poet's grape. It's a finicky plant, your margin of error is tiny, a million things can go wrong, you worry about the weather, but you can get *so* locked into pinot noir. It's the most diverse red wine of all. It makes you think and feel more than other wines. It has grace and power. It has endless nuance. It has an awesome range. It can be pretty and elegant on the one hand or brooding on the other. It can be so light you can just about see through it or so heavy it looks like syrup. Ours leans just a little to the dark side. Not too heavy though. It's balanced. Structure, balance, texture, those are my dad's favorite words. They should be tattooed on my ears by now because I've heard them so many times. You want good color, a rich color, but not too dark, because you want a bright and lively wine. Substantive, a good round feel in the mouth, but not hot— that's what we call a wine with a lot of alcohol. A perfect pinot should be lean on entry, expand in the middle of your palate, be smooth and clean as you swallow, and then linger a little when it's gone. If it lingers too much, if it's big and fat and fruity in your mouth, then it's not freshening your palate. I mean, really, wine should be something that sort of pleasurably cleans your mouth when you eat. It should be enjoyed with food. That's the point. Just drinking wine for itself, well, that's fun for a tasting, or for a glass, but after that what's the point?

Good point, I say, and we walk about another two yards before Jesse says, Man, now I'm all hungry, let's go get lunch and a glass of pinot, which we do, oysters and polenta at the café in town, with a Lange estate reserve pinot noir '99 that he carries in under his arm.

More than half the people in the café say *hey Jesse* as we sit down.

I make him take the first sip of the wine, on the theory that the guy who made the wine should be the judge of its quality, and he swirls it in his glass for a minute, and then deftly rolls his full glass on the table, a cool wine-geek trick I can never quite duplicate, and then he finally takes a sip, straining it back and forth between his teeth, and swallows, and considers, and smiles.

The usual swill? I ask.

*Ex*cellent grapes, he says.

Winemakers of surpassing skill, I say.

Winemakers who know how not to screw up great grapes, he says, artfully dodging, and then the young chef pops over to say *hey Jesse*, and it turns out the young chef and Jesse and a dozen other twentysomethingwinefolk in the valley have regular gatherings at which they taste lots of one kind of wine and at which Jesse is King of the Grill, the Emperor of Sausages, and they just had a riesling gathering in which they tasted almost thirty rieslings, of which the best, says Jesse, were probably the Germans, the Germans are *awful* good at riesling, although of course the New Zealanders are very good at what they do, and there were some very good Oregons there, and you know, he says, there's no reason why Oregon can't make world-class rieslings, we could do it, that's something I think about a lot, if it was up to me we would spend more time on riesling and chardonnay. I mean, we make a good pinot blanc, and a very good riesling, but we make *really* good chardonnay, and that's the grape I'd like to work with, the soil and weather here are just right for a really classy chardonnay, working with the right clones now, the Dijons, not the grassy clones that Oregon started with, that was a mistake, but it's not like there's a *lack* of chardonnay in the world, you know, there's an ocean of the stuff, especially now with California having overplanted like crazy, and the Aussies making it like crazy and selling it for ten cents, so there's no percentage in it for us right now, and anyway our bread and butter is the pinot noir, that's why we're here, that's what we're after, that'll always be our calling card. Pinot noir is why these hills are here, sort of. Or why the vineyards are here on these hills, anyway.

But still, says Jesse, musing, artfully rolling his glass on the table again, I think about chardonnay. Yeh, there's too much chardonnay in the world. But we could make an amazing wine. I think maybe I'll have a little talk with the executive winemaker this afternoon about chardonnay.

THE MOST COMPLICATED &
INTERESTING WINE THERE IS

THE EXECUTIVE WINEMAKER ALWAYS wears a Lange Winery baseball cap. He wears gloves with the fingertips cut off. He is a most cheerful man. I have found him happily wandering through his fig trees, eating new figs with the amazement and zest of a small boy loose in Eden's garden. I have found him happily picking hatfuls of blackberries from the brambled borders of his vineyard. I have found him in his basement happily rooting around for bottles of wine he made fifteen years ago and cannot quite remember where they are although they should dagnabbit be right about here where else could they be it's not like the dang basement is *that* roomy for heaven's sake.

He was born in Marshalltown, Iowa, a village famous for the manufacture of trowels. He was a star quarterback on the high school football team. He didn't much like wine as a young man. He was mostly a beer guy. He wanted to be a writer and earned a degree from the famous University of Iowa Writers' Workshop but by the time he graduated he'd discovered that what he really wanted to write was songs, which he did, eventually composing and recording three albums for Flying Fish Records (*The Same River Twice, Don Lange Live*, and *Natural-Born Heathen*, the last of which was issued in 1978 and dedicated to his infant son Jesse), although, he says, I doubt my records made me more than about ten bucks profit over the course of my career, I don't know if you could possibly stumble into two careers that entail *less* profit for *more* labor than making music and making wine, but I really *like* making music and making wine, so there you are. Or there *I* am, anyways.

In the course of his years of wanderings as a balladeer and star of the peripatetic Don Lange Band he fell in love with California, with the Santa Ynez Valley, with the making of wine, and with a woman named Wendy, who became his wife. He helped out at Sanford & Benedict Vineyard in 1980, exchanging his muscle at harvest for their muscular wine, and then he and Wendy began making wine in their basement, pinot noir and cabernet and merlot and chardonnay, of which the most interesting wine was really the pinot, he says, it's the most complicated and interesting wine there is, you know, but eventually the basement wasn't big enough for the operation we envisioned, so we started looking for land, which was essentially a crazy proposition because we didn't have any money, but we looked anyway, you know how you just keep doing something you want to do even if it doesn't make full sense? Well, we looked at land all around northern California, but just didn't see what we wanted. Then one day we found a bottle of Oregon pinot noir that was . . . unbelievable. The guy who made it, Dick Erath, he had his phone number on the label, and I called him up, and we talked for hours. It turned out that Dick was and is a really great guy and one of the great pioneers of the Oregon wine industry, especially pinot noir, and he convinced us to come look for land in Oregon, so two weeks later we did, and pretty soon we found this property, which it turned out *was* exactly the land we wanted, and it's not all that far from Dick, either, whose winery is just over there a ways.

This hill here, continues Don, had been farmed a long time by the Larsons, Stanley and Catherine Larson, they grew blackcaps, which are black raspberries, which are absolutely delicious, and timber—Douglas fir, mostly, which is not delicious unless you are a beetle. Stanley died a few years ago but Catherine lives in town still. We bought their land in June, cleared and planted in July and August, helped out with harvest in September, bought grapes from our neighbors, and made our first wine in October. That was 1987. There are parts of me that are still sore from 1987. We made that wine in the basement, right here. We made wine down here for three years. Finally we got the barrel room built in 1990, and the winery itself built in 1997, and the tasting room in 1998, but I still have a certain affection for those basement wines. We did pretty well down there. There's a few of those wines in the basement somewhere or other. Remind me to look for them later.

TURTLE ISLAND

THE RICH DEEP RED soil of Dundee, from whence comes what might be the finest pinot noir wine in the world, comes from what were maybe the most stunning floods in the history of the world—the incredible walls of water called variously the Bretz Floods or the Missoula Floods, which thousands of years ago traveled more than sixty miles an hour, carried more than ten times the volume of all the rivers on earth, carved the Columbia River gorge and the coulee canyons of eastern Washington, made the Snake and Willamette rivers run backwards, dropped rocks the size of cottages all over the Pacific Northwest, and filled Oregon's Willamette Valley with soils as deep and rich as any on earth. Again and again and again, some forty times during the Pleistocene Age, walls of icy water two thousand feet high roared across the West from a vast lake in Montana, scouring and sculpting the land, creating lakes a thousand miles across and a thousand feet deep—and leaving behind, on certain hills in Oregon, flood after flood, layer after layer, the basaltic siltish clayish pebblish volcanic loam so beloved of the pinot noir vine.

Called Jory soil, after Jory Hill near Salem where the stuff is especially noticeable, it is generally four to six feet deep, relatively porous, high in iron (whence cometh the reddish-orange-coppery-rusty color), and layered like a dessert on the basaltic bedrock laid down over millennia by the volcanoes of the nearby Cascade range. The volcanic and porous nature of the dirt in the Red Hills (as opposed to the sedimentary and water-retaining soils in the lower valley, which can be more than a hundred feet deep) means that it drains quickly—a crucial virtue with the fussy fidgety pinot noir vine, which, as Jesse says, hates to get its feet wet.

Jory soil is so localized and identifiable in the Willamette Valley that it has officially been named Oregon's state soil— dirt that is ours alone, like the proud dirts of Idado (Threebear), Maine (Chesuncook), and New Mexico (Penistaja). In recent years each of the United States has declared indigenous dirts, and their names are a poem of this sweet and salty land: Myakka and Menfro, Marlow and Monongahela, Hilo and Hazelton, Natchez and Narragansett, Bayamon and Bohicket, Honeoye and Houston, Miami and Mivida, Tifton and Tama, Stuttgart and Seitz, Drummer and Downer, Harney and Scobey, Tama and Antigo and Pamunkey and Oravada and Antigo and Estelle and o the song of soils draped on what the first peoples wandering across the continent came to call Turtle Island—the great tortoise on which is layered the soil from which the Lakota people say human beings emerged, dirty faces first, blinking in the morning sun.

ICE WINE

JANUARY. I WANDER UP to the vineyard, my car laboring and skidding up the icy road, and find six inches of snow on the ground and chaos in the winery. The emergency of the moment is that the café in town has run out of Lange pinot noir and placed an order for twenty-five cases from the distributor, but the distributor can't get his gargantuan truck up the hill to the winery because the road is such a mess, which is why Don is muttering darkly about fraudulent and incompetent county commissioners, and Jesse grills me about the condition of the road, and minutes later a cavalcade of five cars and pickup trucks from the winery carry five cases of pinot noir each down the hill to town, and I alone am left to tell thee that I was once, for an hour on a silent winter morning, in sole command of a noted Oregon winery, which was pretty cool.

It's not like you'll actually get anybody in the tasting room today, says Jesse, grinning, so don't break anything, don't fix anything, and don't make any wine, either. It'd probably be best if you just stood right there and didn't move. Don't answer the phone. Keep an eye on the dogs. Stay out of the barrel room. We'll bring back lunch.

Which they do, an hour later, their trucks and cars swerving and spraying mud and snow, and we all sit huddled in the winery, pillars of breath rising in the moist air, eating fish sandwiches with a crisp dry German riesling that Don found in his basement. A lovely wine, the clean chalky flavor perfect with tartar sauce.

It's so cold in the winery, and the German wine is so brisk and clean, that the words *ice wine* pops into my mind, and I ask Don if he's ever made ice wine, a late-harvest wine made from grapes pressed after they freeze on the vine.

Well, sort of, he says darkly, and Jesse chortles, and they explain that at harvest three years ago they decided to make a late-harvest riesling, which they did, leaving the riesling grapes on the vine until they froze, and that was a very good wine if I don't say so myself, says Don, but the bottling machine broke as we were finishing the bottling of that particular wine, and while we were fixing the machine some yeast developed on the filter, but we didn't know that at the time, and only discovered it when after a few months some of the late-harvest riesling fermented *in the bottle*, producing, for the first and so far only time in Lange Winery history, a sparkling wine. Which we didn't sell, considering it was a mistake, but it was actually pretty good stuff. We gave it away as gifts. I think there are three or four cases left in the basement.

That was a phenomenal wine, says Jesse. We should make more mistakes.

We did make another late-harvest riesling, last year, he continues, and believe you me we kept a close eye on the bottling machine, and that's a very good wine, but I'm not sure we'll do that again. I have been thinking about getting out of riesling altogether. It's getting in the way of the chardonnay and pinot gris, and those are the white grapes we should be growing here. Plus I wouldn't mind experimenting with other grapes, like gewurztraminer.

We could do something interesting with tempranillo, I bet, says Don. But you can only have so many experiments going on at the same time, and we have a lot of experiments going on at the moment.

We finish the German riesling and everyone sits quietly for a moment, Don humming, and then, as if on some silent signal, they all rise at once and return to work among tool

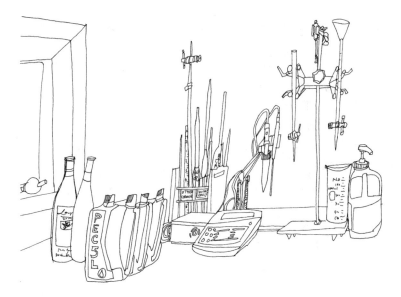

chests, hoses, pallets, boxes, smocks, boots, hand-trucks, jackets, crates, mops, dogs, tanks, corks, casks, rakes, the bottling machine, the labeling machine, the fluttering pages of purchase orders tacked to the wall.

Chuy's plan for the afternoon, he tells me shyly, is to clean the biggest of the steel tanks, and I watch as he dons a slicker and rubber boots and folds himself gently through the tank's porthole, closing the door after him like a man closing a submarine hatch. A minute later the hatch opens quietly and his hand emerges and feels around on the floor for his mop and then withdraws, with the mop, back into the silver belly of the tank.

A SPECK OF RED DUST

A FTER DAVID AND DIANA LETT came the deluge in
Oregon: Dick and Kena Erath, and Cal Knudsen, and
Dick and Nancy Ponzi, and Susan and Bill Sokol Blosser, and
David and Ginny Adelsheim, and Chuck and Shirley Coury,
and Jim and Donna McDaniel, and Sally Bauers, and Bill
Fuller, and Joe and Pat Campbell, and Ron and Marge
Vuylsteke, and Ken and Penny Durant, and Richard Sommer,
and Frank Wisnovsky, and Jim Maresh and Arthur Weber, and
many more, and they planted hill after hill of pinot noir on
what had been hazelnut orchard and apple orchard and cherry
orchard and plum orchard and stands of fir and brambles of
berry, and in 1979 the Letts' Eyrie pinot noir was famously
ranked ahead of Burgundy's best in a Paris tasting, and by 1980
there were enough passionate pinot noir nuts in Oregon to call
an annual summer meeting of the clan on the Umpqua River to
taste and discuss and argue and deal and learn. (They also, that
summer, discussed the effect of fresh-fallen volcanic ash on
grape leaves, a pressing concern as of the morning of May 18,
when Mount Saint Helens in Washington state exploded and
showered up to three inches of ash on Oregon.)

By the end of the 1980s there were a thousand acres of
Oregon under pinot vine; by the turn of the century there were
five thousand acres nestling noir, a number expected to double
again by 2010. And Burgundy came to Oregon also: Robert
Drouhin, of the ancient House of Joseph Drouhin of Beaune,
bought a hundred-acre hillside in the Red Hills of Dundee in
1987 and established Domain Drouhin Oregon. Nearly two
decades after one of the oldest and most prestigious French
winemakers invested in a hill a mile from the Langes, there are

350 wineries in Oregon, more than fourteen thousand acres of the state under vine, and an annual crush of 20,000 tons. Today Oregon ranks second in the nation in number of wineries (behind California), annually produces more than a million cases of wine (more than half of which is pinot noir), and sells its wine for more than a hundred million dollars a year.

Well, says Jesse, yeh, that *sounds* impressive, a hundred million dollars a year, but Oregon's share of the national market for all wines sold is about 1 percent, and Oregon's share of the *world* market for all wines sold is a speck of red dust. So far. Our calling card, and the future, and what is putting us on the world wine map, is pinot noir, and that's right and true and apt and fair, and that will only be more true as we get better and better at it and make more of it and more people worldwide get hip to our wines, but me, personally, myself, I think part of the future for us is also pinot gris. I mean, those are the two wines that *are* Oregon. I can see the license plates in 2030: Oregon, Pinot Paradise. And there's something ironic about that, isn't there? I mean, here we are, a state that for the longest time was known for timber and salmon, home-grown products rising up out of the land and water, and basically we wiped out those products, but in the future we will almost certainly be known for another home-grown product that rises up out of the land and water, one that is endlessly renewable and sustainable and environmentally stewardly and all, one that reflects the agricultural bent of the state and its people and history, and respect for the land, and intelligent responsible land use, and attentiveness to the natural world, and the entrepreneurial itch, and the urge for communal enterprise, all the stuff that we think of as very Oregonian. Which is pretty cool.

I see you've thought about this a little, I say.

Just a little, he says, grinning.

SHEETS & SQUALLS

F EBRUARY. A STEADY RAIN falls and has always fallen and
will always fall and the prospect of it not falling ever again
is incomprehensible and inconceivable and impossible. I stand
at the rattling winery windows and watch the sheets and squalls
of rain, and remember the Ray Bradbury story about a planet
where it rains all day every day except for one hour a year.

Okay, off we go, says Jesse, donning his jacket and not
even putting on a hat.

What—out there? In that?

Aw, it's not as bad as usual, says Jesse. C'mon, I'll teach you
about grafting and pruning.

Off we trudge into the old pinot block, avoiding puddles
the size of oceans, Jesse shouting into the howling rain, Time to
prune! There are fifteen hundred plants per acre! We wait until
after the chance of frost and then we tell them essentially where
to go! The plants are fully dormant now, they're curled up for
the winter, and now we set the table for the growing season!

The wind is blowing so hard and there's so much rain that
the rain is really and truly coming at us sideways, which you
hardly ever see. I try to remember when I have ever been so
thoroughly wet before while clothed and can only remember
one time many years ago when I went on a whale watch that
turned out to be a more of a gale watch, during which not only
were there no whales to be seen at all in the least, not a wisp or
whisper of whale whatsoever, but certainly any whale in the
area resident or transient was huddled shivering in an
underwater pub somewhere away from all the howling rain.

Jesse crouches down and deftly whips vine canes up and
around the lowest of the four rows of wire and shows me how to
train the canes that will be this year's grape factories along the

wires, and he shows me how he and his work crew will prune
with an eye toward next year's canes as well, two-year canes, he
calls them, which are, at this soggy moment, mere bumps on the
stalk of the vine, and we also talk for a while, in the wild wailing
wet, about grafting, which he and Don had to do one year for
complicated reasons, and grafting turns out to be an adventure
and a half! shouts Jesse into the rain, because you basically
decapitate the vine you don't want, leaving the thick stalk, and
then you carry the cuttings of the vine you *do* want in holsters
down to the vine you *don't* want, and cut holes in the vine you
don't want and insert the cuttings of the vine you *do* want and
then wrap the whole thing in a special tape so it can breathe but
be protected against bugs and fungus and all, and then you have
to come back to it regularly and cut water holes because the
vine you *don't* want is so freaking vigorous, and is hauling up so
much water through its root system, that if you don't watch out
it will push the cuttings right back out, so you wander around
with a saw cutting water holes, which heal fast, vines are tough!

I remark, shouting, the subtle irony of cutting water holes
in creatures (a) drenched on a regular basis by gobs of rain like
today and (b) legendary for millennia for finding water in the
most stony stark bleak unforgiving frowning land, and Jesse
says yeh, grapevines are amazing life forms when you think
about it, they plunge their fingers a hundred feet down into
the rocky soil, they can live for hundreds of years, they fend
off all sorts of insect attacks, and they have been working with
human beings so long, thousands and thousands of years, that
you wonder sometimes who cultivates who, you know what I
mean? Are people manipulating and taking advantage of
grape vines, or are grape vines deftly using human beings to
take over the world?

Good question, I shout.

Think about it, shouts Jesse. And are we done here now?
Because this is crazy to be out in rain like this. Let's go get a beer.

PLANT A BON VIN

FEBRUARY. WHAT WITH THE steady rain falling and endlessly falling and the prospect of the world forever being gray and misty and wet and moist and drumming gently with sheets and walls and curtains of rain fondling every inch of the hills and rills and curves and swerves of Oregon, what with the rain falling silver and dark, falling obliquely against the dim winter light, falling on every part of every parking lot, falling softly upon the vineyards and hazelnut orchards, softly falling into the deep red soil, falling thickly through the universe and faintly falling on all the living and the dead, I spend a lot of time indoors reading about wine, and I discover that more Americans drink wine now than at any time in the history of America. They drink more white wine than red. They drink more varietals—wines made from one kind of grape, like chardonnay—than ever before. Twenty years ago 20 percent of table wine bought in America was varietal; today it is 80 percent. The most popular varietals are chardonnay, cabernet, and merlot. Pinot noir is a fast-rising but still tiny player in America, except in Oregon. Women buy more wine than men and drink more wine than men. Most people who drink wine regularly have at least a dozen bottles in their homes, and of those dozen or more bottles most are chardonnay, cabernet, and merlot. Pinot noir is a peanut saleswise. By percentage, on average, an American who drinks wine regularly will have about an eighth of a bottle of pinot noir in his or her home—about half a glass.

Being an American who drinks wine regularly, I check my wine cellar, which isn't in the cellar and has hardly any wine in it: three bottles, I discover, two of which are untouchable triumphs reserved for momentous celebration, and the third a wonderfully cheap Italian wine suitable for pouring with pizza. My wine cellar is a rickety wooden rack perched on the mantel, a rack I put together my own personal self with the wrong glue some years ago when my lovely research assistant and I had a rebellious three-year-old daughter and then, overnight, brand-new wailing infant howling twin sons. I have a vague memory of gluing the rack together shortly after the arrival of Chaos and Hubbub as an act of faith in a future that would include bottles of wine and the time to sip them; a future that has sort of arrived, in that now I get to drink a glass of wine every night with dinner, but then I have to help *some*one with his math homework, or help someone *else* with *his* project about Viking ships that's due *tomorrow morning*, and he for*got* to tell dad about it because *dad* flagrantly and egregiously *forgot* to *remind* his son to *tell* his dad about the project so this is all technically *dad's* fault (wailing, recriminations, gnashing of teeth), then I assist in wrangling dishes and laundry and tardy homeworkers to bed, and then I am hectored and lectured by the now-lanky former three-year-old about *her* shower schedule in the morning, which takes precedence over all *other* shower schedules for reasons that are murky to me, and by that time it's really too late to drink more wine, so I *read* about wine, which is in a strange way almost as pleasant as drinking wine, and I become absorbed in the history of wine, which interestingly actually includes Viking ships carrying barrels of wine, but also may include extinct species of plants shouldered aside after millions of years by the genetic winner of the race, *Vitis vinifera*, which is cousin to ivy, and which used to grow wild ten thousand years ago, and still does, but somewhere along the historical line, perhaps ten thousand years ago, some enterprising soul planted a bud or a cutting from a wild vine, and discovered that the cutting grew into an exact genetic copy of the parent vine; and so began the complicated and entertaining craft, industry, and cultural phenomenon of winemaking.

The earliest traces of the craft, as the scholar John Haeger notes dryly, are "stubbornly obscure," but shards of pottery and cups bearing the chemical residue of fermented grape juice, and dating back as far as six thousand years, have been found around the Mediterranean and in Iran, Iraq, and Egypt. Pinot noir itself is thought to have arisen in the Cote d'Or some two centuries before Christ; a Spaniard euphoniously named Lucilius Junius Moderatus Columella, in the first years after the death of the gaunt Jewish rebel Yesuah ben Joseph in Jerusalem, lauds a small savory Burgundian grape variety with particularly rounded leaves, a notable tolerance for cold temperatures, and the virtue of improving the longer it was left in barrel or bottle—all characteristics of pinot noir.

By the fourteenth century after Christ the grape sometimes called *pynos* or *pineau* or *noirien* or *pinot* or *plant noble* was mentioned commonly in Burgundy, where it was also, entertainingly, called *plant a bon vin,* plant of the good wine, and it has remained the great grape of Burgundy ever since; today there are more than twenty thousand acres of *plant a bon vin* in the Cote d'Or, Cote Chalonnaise, and Maconnais regions of Burgundy alone, not to mention a raft of other regions in France and Germany and Italy and Serbia and Montenegro and Macedonia and Romania and Switzerland and Austria and Bulgaria and Hungary and Slovakia and the Czech Republic and New Zealand and Australia and South Africa and Chile and China and Japan. And Oregon.

THE GOLDEN WEST

M ARCH. I WANDER UP to the winery and talk to Wendy, who tells me that she was born in Connecticut but yearned for California and finally arrived in the golden west where she met Don and soon found herself teaching grade school during the day and making wine in the basement at night, merlot cabernet chardonnay and of *course* pinot noir, she says, considering who my husband is. You could legitimately say, she says, that Lange Winery began there in our basement in California, because that's where we started the process of getting bonded with the federal Bureau of Alcohol, Tobacco, and Firearms, which you need to do to make and sell wine.

I note that federal registration of winemaking harks back all the way to 1791 when the first Congress stuck a tax on any and all spirits made in this country, which they did to pay off debts from the war against England, so it's interesting to think, I say, that the registration and taxing of wineries in America are traceable to paying for a rebellion against the empire two centuries ago.

We talk for a while about wine and war, and how Americans through history have had a complicated relationship with spirits in general, wines originally being something you would make in the normal course of the farm year, dandelion wine and elderberry wine and cherry wine and blackberry wine, in the same way you would make applejack and corn whiskey, and we talk about how wines were initially marketed as medicine and soothing-syrups and aphrodisiacs and such, and how wine also entered the culture through the religion of immigrants from Ireland and the daily diets of immigrants from Italy, and how some grapegrowers and winemakers mostly in California survived the *thirteen years* of Prohibition by selling grape juice or making wine for Catholic sacramental use, and how wine in America had, by the end of the twentieth century, grown past cult status into cultural status in popular films and travel destinations and, perhaps most reflective of true and heartfelt American admiration, real estate prices, and this line of talk brings Wendy back to the land at hand, the soil under sole, the dirt in her heart.

So then, she says, as Don probably explained, we looked for land in California, but nothing was quite right, but then we found this place, where the Larsons grew raspberries, and it was ex*act*ly right, so here we are, and have been since 1987.

What was it like before you had the winery?

Well, we were making wine in the basement, which gets old fast, especially in Oregon when from November through May it's cold and wet, and there's nowhere on earth colder and wetter and muddier in winter than a basement in rural Oregon. So I was thrilled when we finally built the winery. That's when the mud finally stopped coming in the house. But when we started we were also our own distributors, of course, so I would be up at four in the morning to deliver our wine to stores. That's when loading docks open. And then I'd have to be back up here at eleven in the morning to open the tasting room. There were a few days there when I was in bed right after dinner. There were a few days there when I was in bed *before* dinner. There were a few days there when I was so tired I couldn't drink a glass of the wine we were making, which seemed a little . . . ironic.

THE BOAR TAGLIATELLE

M ARCH. MY SUBTLE WIFE reminds me of the first time we actually personally met Jesse, which was some years ago and interestingly not, as she notes, in his vineyard, but at a dark back table in a fancy restaurant in Dundee, where we were celebrating a wedding anniversary and hiding for a night from the three headlong products of the wedding, and where Jesse was at the time a waiter, because, as he told me later, he was fresh out of college, didn't have ten cents, it was winter and the winery was slow, he knew his wines, and the owner of the restaurant was his dad's college roommate, so he got hired as a waiter until he tired as a waiter, and went back up to the winery to eventually become general manager and winemaker, and be peppered with projects and questions by such quizzical creatures as me.

That whole evening comes back to me now—the wit and zest of my research assistant, the swirl and swing of conversation, the dense earthy mushroom soup, the spicy boar tagliatelle, the nearby table conversations tendrilling by, you know how you catch scraps and shards of conversations from other tables, just the tail-ends, often just a few enticing words like *mistress* or *misdemeanor*, and I remember the excellent wine, a pinot noir suggested by our waiter, a courteous young man with a Lange corkscrew in his pocket. We had asked his advice on wine, specifying only that it be a local pinot noir, and he thought for a moment and then recommended a wine from a vineyard about twelve miles southwest of our table.

My sharp-eyed bride noted his corkscrew and asked its provenance, and the polite young waiter explained that he personally himself was a Lange, the scion of the Lange estate,

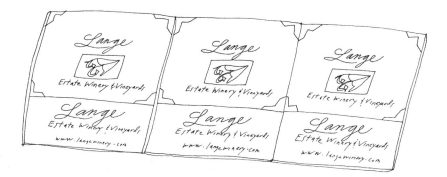

such as it muddily was, and
he recommended, in his gentlemanly way,
that at some point we stop by the estate for a taste of their
wines if we had a loose hour or so, as he could attest to the
quality of the wines, having helped make them.

I reminded him of this episode, years later, and asked him
why he had recommended another winery's wine to us that
night when he could very easily have recommended his own.

Because I am not a total sales geek, he said, and on that
wine list at that time there were, as I remember, maybe five
pinot noirs that went well with the boar, which was slightly
too salty, in my opinion, so I probably recommended a wine
that would stand up to the salt. What did I recommend?

I name the wine, which I remember partly because I am
memorious and partly for its admirable burliness.

Yeh, that's a very good pinot, but a little too heavy, said
Jesse. Our wine is better balanced. That's very well made,
though. You have to be fair about the quality of other wines.
There are some really terrific pinot noirs made here in the
valley.

Like which? I ask.

O no, he says, grinning. No no. Nice try. I like everybody.

FAUX PAX

M ARCH. I WANDER UP to the vineyard and Jesse and I go over numbers and maps and delivery schedules and production records and shipping orders and supply records and sales projections and marketing plans and such. We start with the grapes. The grapes that make up Lange's wines come from seven vineyards in Oregon, one of which is the rilled hill on which we stand.

This hill, says Jesse, grows pinot noir, chardonnay, some white grape we are not totally sure what it is in a row at the bottom of the hill near the fence, and one time something which we *thought* was pinot noir, we bought seedlings that were supposed to be pinot noir, but it turns out they *weren't* pinot noir, which was a bit of a problem.

What was it?

Cabernet sauvignon. We had a little chat with the seller about that.

You made a cabernet? I ask, surprised; the very idea of pinot noir people making cabernet sauvignon is a little startling, like a dancer suddenly taking up kick-boxing.

We didn't think it would be much of a wine, says Jesse. This isn't the place for cabernet. But we made it anyway just to see what would happen.

What happened?

It was . . . interesting. We called it Faux Pax.

Was it any good?

It was . . . drinkable.

Does it still exist?

We actually sold it all, pretty much as a joke, says Jesse. People thought it was funny that there *was* such a thing as a

Lange cabernet. I bet my dad has a few bottles down in the basement, though.

We talk about the other Oregon hills that grow the grapes that make Lange wines. They are all within twenty miles of the winery. They are all owned by men and women the Langes trust with a deep and abiding trust. They are all on renewable contracts. One has been delivering grapes to Lange Winery since the first summer there was such a thing as Lange Winery, seventeen years ago. The newest has been delivering grapes to Lange for four years. Two years ago the Langes took those grapes from this newish vineyard and made a single-vineyard wine from it, partly, says Jesse, at the request of the grower, who is a cheerful man the size of a cottage, and partly as an agricultural vinicultural viticultural oenological experiment, because that vineyard is relatively high up in the Coast Range mountains, on the western wall of the valley, above the headwaters of the Tualatin River, and Don in particular, being an experimentalish-minded man, wanted to see what a west-wall-of-the-valley wine would taste like.

What does it taste like? I ask.

Clove, oranges, cocoa, sage, plums, cherries, and a grain of allspice in the nose, says Jesse promptly, and not for the first time and not for the last I think to myself that one of the cooler things in life is meeting people who like what they do and are good at what they do and are doing exactly the thing that they should be doing at that particular time; a rare and delightful symmetry and synchronicity in a world so often mostly shatter and rattle and shiver and smash.

TENDRILLING

CONSIDER THE ARCHITECTURE OF a grape. At the head,
so to speak, is the pedicel, or stem, which connects the
individual berry to its brothers and sisters in the cluster.
Through the pedicel flow nutrients from the rest of the plant—
water and minerals, most of which are drawn up to the berry
by the vigorous roots, which are so eager and energetic and
businesslike that they can grow an inch a day. The berry is
bounded by its skin, or exocarp, which protects the pulp,
which in turn protects what the grape itself would consider the
crown jewel of the operation, the incipient baby, the embryo,
the endosperm, the glorious future: the seed. The seed could,
of course, give birth to a whole new pinot noir vine, but most of
the time it doesn't, because the vast majority of new plantings
in a vineyard are cuttings from other plants, and the vast
majority of the seeds produced by all the pinot noir vines in the
world every year go spinning into fermenters along with skins.

At Lange, after the fermented juice is drained away from
the crush, the seeds and skins (after five days in the fermenter,
a redolent shriveled dried black muck like grape jerky or grape
granola) are thrown on the compost heap in the sunny
southwest corner of the vineyard. Sometimes a vine will start
up back there out of the heap and the Langes just let it grow,
mostly because they have a lot of other things to do and could
not care less about wild pinot vines but also, concedes Jesse,
on the vague theory that you never know, the vines that pop
out of seeds back there might be the best grapes you ever saw.

Whyn't you plant a few and see what'll happen? I suggest,
realizing as soon as I utter the words that I am actually
proposing more work for someone else to do, always bad form
in this galaxy.

Hmm, says Jesse, well,
we have about a hundred experiments going
on around here already, so I don't think we are going
to get around to it, myself, but, you know, if *you* have some
loose time on your hands, be my guest.

I stand by the compost heap and look respectfully at the
wild vines tendrilling and writhing toward the oak trees by the
house, and I remember what Jesse told me once about the mad
creativity of the pinot noir vine; that it is considered the most
genetically unstable of all grape plants, and that while a
cabernet vine may produce as many as forty different
mutations, a pinot noir vine can make more than ten thousand.
I ponder cutting seedlings from these wild vines and planting
them around my house, which is something I always thought
would be pretty cool, especially in Oregon, having pinot noir
vines as part of your yard, but then I have visions of snarling
mutant pinot noir vines as thick as biker arms growing taller
than the house, and smashing their gnarled fists through the
windows and opening the refrigerator and drinking my beer
and smoking my cigars and playing rap music really loud and
kidnapping small yappy neighbor dogs and such, and I back
away slowly from the compost heap and wander back up to the
winery, feeling unaccountably that something is watching me.

WINEWORDS

ARCH. WALLY AND I get to talking about the word *clone*, which is, says Wally, his spectacles glinting in the moist afternoon light, from the Greek word for twig, *klon*, and this, you know, he says, is perfectly apt and suitable, because every vine is propagated from sprouted bud wood, a twig taken from another vine, never from seed, so the term *clone* has come to be applied to what really is a *twig*. Which is interesting.

It turns out that both of us are wordheads absorbed by the weird poetry of What Words Come From What Other Words and we get to talking about the etymology of all sorts of winewords, from the word *wine* itself, which comes from the Old English word *win,* which comes from the Old Germanic word *winam,* which comes from the Latin word *vinum*, which some etymologists think comes from a lost ancient word something like *woin,* which was probably born along the Mediterranean somewhere and then was poured into all sorts of languages, like the Norse *vin,* and the Dutch *wijn*, and the modern German *wein,* and the Italian *vino,* and the Lithuanian *vynas,* and the Welsh *gwin,* and the Gaelic *fin,* and we talk about the word *grape*, which is, interestingly, a French word, harking from *graper,* to pick grapes, which was an Old German word that itself came from the even older German words *krappon* and *krapfo,* which both meant the tool that you would use to pick grape clusters.

Somewhere in the vast disordered sea of my reading, I say, I remember noticing that the Old English word for grape was *winberige*, and Wally says Ah, now, that's apt and suitable too because you can hear what that word means, *wine berry*, which is what of course the grape is.

And we discuss the word *vintage*, which comes from the
Old French word *vendage*, meaning yield from the vineyard,
which itself comes from the Latin word *vindemia*, a gathering
of grapes, and we discuss odd wine words like *zinfandel*, which
no one knows where it comes from, and *shiraz*, which is a city
in Iran, and *marsala*, which is a city in Sicily, and *chianti*, which
is a range of mountains in Italy, and *moselle*, which is a river in
Germany, and *chardonnay* and *champagne* and *cognac*, all of
which are districts in France, and *tokay*, which is a city in
Hungary, and *sherry*, which word comes from the city of Jerez
in Spain, and *gourmet*, which comes ultimately from the French
word *grommes*, or wine-tasters, and the word *ton*, which comes
from *tun*, which is an old English word that meant the space
occupied by a cask of wine, and the word *libation*, which is
from the Latin word *libationem*, which meant the wine you
would pour as an offering to the gods, so the more closely we
look, says Wally professorially, we see that there are an amazing
number of words with wine tangled in their histories, which is
fascinating, all things considered, and now, speaking of wine
and wineries, I really must get back to work, though this has
been a pleasant etymological interlude, for which thanks.

What's the project of the day? I ask.

Projects plural, as always, says Wally. Today is a bottling
and labeling day and then there will be six or seven other small
but pressing projects that will need attention. And something
will probably break down and need attention.

Attention, I say, from the Latin word *attendere*, to give
heed to or to stretch toward, like to stretch your mind toward
something. The word is used that way in Chaucer, as I
remember from a class I had about a thousand years ago.

Ah, enough, says Wally, grinning. I have to stretch my
mind toward the bottling machine. Go away now.

ANTIPODIAD

MARCH. I WANDER ALL the way down to Australia on a
bookish tour but I swear and vow to Jesse beforehand
that I will taste Oznoirs while Antipodean so I make a
concerted effort to do so, as a sort of secret field agent for
Lange Winery abroad, and I talk up Lange's wines to my
hosts, and to my friends there, and to people near me at an
Australian Rules football game between the Geelong Cats and
the Saint Kilda Saints, and to the tiny gracious Greek man
who makes me coffee every morning and hands it to me silent
and grinning and bowing, and to people on the city tram who
look at me oddly, and to the quiet Chinese woman who hands
me Anzac biscuits every afternoon, and I even take notes on
Ozwines in my little moleskin notebook, which makes my
Australian friends grin their sunny grins.

I taste pinot noirs while eating kangaroo filets on the
Mornington Peninsula south of Melbourne in a vineyard that
slopes down gently into a bay filled with water that was
recently sliding past Antarctica. I taste pinot noirs in a tiny
courtyard in the bubbling seething singing shaggy Fitzroy
district of Melbourne. I have a mouthful of pinot noir in the
middle of the vast grass sea of Carlton Gardens with a young
couple sprawled on the grass who pour a second splash into the
plastic cup they give me *because,* says the young man with a
sunny grin, *yer country produced Springsteen for which we owe ya.* I
have a glass of pinot noir under the new stars deep in the dry
red dusty country listening to birds I never heard before late at
night under an ironbark tree. I have a glass of pinot noir sitting
on a hot stone wall by the Yarra River as a young rugby team
from Warrnambool runs by. I taste pinot noirs on the quay by

the Opera House as the city of Sydney sets off fireworks over the harbor. I have a glass of pinot noir in the thick muggy ardent fervid dense dusk of the Botanical Gardens amid figs and cypress and lovers and ibis and moorhens and cockatoos and she-oaks and banksias as a vast river of fruit bats flows by above me and swirls around the golden turrets of the old cathedral. I have a glass of pinot noir late in the afternoon on a brilliant day in a tiny seaside bar on Manly Beach, sitting there barefoot and shirtless and smiling, little kids on the beach giggling and yowling, mynah birds arguing over french fries, a currawong moaning piteously in a nearby jacaranda tree.

When I get back to America and wander up to the winery Jesse asks me Hey, how were the wines in Australia? and I find myself suddenly speechless, unable to articulate how the wines I sipped in that wide cheerful light actually *were* that brilliant country and its riveting people to me, the grin of the young man sprawled in the park with his shy girlfriend, the fireworks over the dark velvety starry harbor, the black and white schoolboys running past me laughing on their way to the gleaming green gem of the rugby field, the headlong arrowing of red and green parrots through gum trees, the tiny cups of ferocious dense black coffee, the small shrill brown girls kicking a football hilariously on the beach, the zest and dust and hope and dirt and verve and sun and salt of that land, the swirling voices talking to me in their cheerful language of their country's sins and sadnesses and sports and wars and joys and possibility and poetry and pain and pinot noir.

It was . . . unbelievable, I tell Jesse. It's hard to explain.

I dig, he says, looking at me closely.

PINOT NOIR FOR BURROS

APRIL. A MOIST PREGNANT day, dense with wet expectation.

Okay, I say to Jesse, pretend I don't know anything whatsoever about how to make pinot noir, which I don't, and walk me from grape to bottle in about three minutes. You're the teacher and I am the entire enrollment in Pinot Noir for Burros.

Okay, says Jesse. We pick the grapes. We run them through the stemmer, which takes the stems off. We run them through the crusher-destemmer, which crushes them gently and separates juice from skins and seeds. We put juice and seeds and skins in the fermenting bins, where they ferment for a few days, with us shoving the whole muck around usually three times a day to get every possible scrap of color and flavor, and then we put this whole gluck in the press, which yields just the juice, which is now raw wine, and we throw all the dry seeds and skins out on the compost heap and barrel the new wine. Once it's in barrel it settles, which means any particulates or impurities settle to the bottom of the cask, which clarifies the wine, which is what you want, because no one wants to drink muddy wine. Remember the raw wine we had that one day right from the cask, that looked like a cloudy day in the glass? That's what was happening there, the wine hadn't settled yet. So then over the next twelve or fifteen or eighteen months or so we test the pinot in barrel, and lift it off the settlings, which are called lees, and the wines are during those months also going through a second fermentation in the barrel, called maloactic fermentation, which essentially smoothes the wine and makes it more complex. You ever have any chemistry in college?

Nope.

High school?

Nope.

No chemistry at all ever? Geez.

Nope, I say. I studied basketball and books, basically. And girls. You?

Philosophy, business, chemistry, botany. And girls. Lifetime study, girls.

There's a subject let's run screaming away from, says Jesse. Well, anyway, take my word for it, maloactic fermentation occurs in the barrel and it's a good thing. So we keep tasting and testing and then when the wines are mature we decide what to blend with what and which barrels to use for the single-vineyard wines, and then we bottle the wines, and cork them, and label them, and have a release party, and ship off some to people who already bought them as futures, and sell the rest, except for a few cases that end up in the basement every year. I think we have at least a few bottles of every wine we ever made, which is a heck of a thing so say, because over eighteen years we have made way more than a hundred different wines. Some by accident, like the Faux Pas and the sparkling wine. So, okay, you get the system?

Yeh, I say. It sounds so deceptively simple. Get grapes, crush grapes, barrel juice, wait a year.

But o the million things that can go wrong, says Jesse. And everything going right depends completely on the grapes, which let's go check on them, and we amble off down the hill into the exuberant green rows.

TASTELESS

APRIL. I GET SO mindbogglingly howlingly bedraggledly mournfully sick with the flu and then pneumonia and then pneumonia *again* that I spend two weeks in bed moaning and hacking and pondering my early demise and worrying about the children and wondering how in heaven's name my poor research assistant is ever going to raise three children and a puppy by herself, and I have vast inchoate fever dreams and cannot eat or drink or sleep for days and days, and I am so sick that I lose interest in love and light and music and books and laughter, and at the nadir of what feels like the plague from the fourth circle of hell I call my doctor and beg to be sent to the hospital and be sedated and put in an oxygen tent, which she declines to do for reasons that are murky to me, and finally after what feels like nine months I emerge mewling from the bed and spend the next two weeks pale and shadowy and gaunt, and I shakily begin to drink tea and eat saltines and slices of apple, things that have never tasted so good to me in forty years, and finally I feel enough like the man I used to be that I think a tiny sip of excellent pinot gris will be Just The Thing, a mouthful of clean crisp clear Lange pinot gris (2001, a good year) will be restorative, it will be medicine straight from the soil of my region of the world, it will remind my body that wine maketh merry the heart, it will revive and restore and resurrect some cheerful part of me, and I take a sip and *it tastes horrendous!* it tastes like the worst foul liquid ever inflicted on an unsuspecting innocent! it tastes like some evil mix of castor oil and motor oil and curse words! it tastes so unbelievably mindbendingly awful that I dash it into the sink and reach for the whole bottle to dash *that* into the sink

before my alert wife says *whoa there, bub* and I say, nearly
weeping with the shock of *Jesse's wine tasting horrible!* an idea
that has never entered my mind before as even remotely
possible! that the bottle must have gone bad! and my wife,
intelligent creature that she be, tastes the wine and says, um,
no, this is terrific wine, and I realize with horror that that my
taste buds have given up the collective ghost—I have become
that which I always feared to be, tasteless.

My face must have registered my shock and dismay and
the way this all felt like totally unfair insult added to the
actual injury of being howlingly sick for a whole month,
because my wife, who is a perceptive soul, says, trying not to
smile, It's only temporary, you know, because you have been
taking gobs of antibiotics and other medicines and your
mouth is all out of whack, it'll pass, don't worry, you only have
another couple of weeks of antibiotics, and I stand there all
mournful for a while thinking two more *weeks* without any
wine at *all*, and I feel like a big baby, but I actually really *like* a
glass of wine every day, it's just a fact, and I make a manful
effort to look at this startling state of affairs as a chance to
take a vacation from wine, a sensible idea for anyone every
once in a while, wine is after all an alcoholic liquid, one does
well to abstain occasionally not only from wine but from any
habit, habits being the slippery slopes to routines and ruts,
and I get so tired thinking about habits and ruts, and trying to
convince myself that it's a good thing not to be able to drink
wine, that I have to go lie down, sighing quietly.

PINOT PIERRE

A PRIL. I WANDER UP to the vineyard and find Jesse with a new and startlingly thick beard, which is sort of unnerving in that I keep feeling I am talking to a young Herman Melville or Walt Whitman about vintages and clones and such, but after the obligatory moment of male razzing we talk about the vegetative architecture of the vineyard, as it were—what's where and why.

Because of the angle of the hillside, he says, there's the big central plot and then the two smaller side plots. Let's start with the central plot. The rows are planted on a north-south orientation, about six feet apart, with about eighteen rows per clone. So at the top of the hill, rows 1 to 18, that's pinot noir, Wadenswil clone, and then, in descending order down the hill, in rows 19 through 33 pinot noir Bien Nacido, in rows 34 to 48 pinot noir Pommard, and then plots of pinot noir clone 115, pinot noir 114, chardonnay Dijon clone, and the mysterious white grape in a row by the fence.

What is that?

Not sure. It's a mutant. We know what it's not—not chardonnay, not pinot gris, not pinot blanc, not reisling. We're calling it Pinot Pierre because we bought it from a guy named Peter Gladheart. Should have fruit next year.

You'll make a wine?

Yeh—there should be enough for at least one barrel. We'll see.

What are the side plots? I ask.

On this side, right out in front of the winery, there's the new block, about forty rows of pinot noir 777 clone, probably my favorite pinot noir to work with, and then below that is chardonnay, clone 76, and below that nothing, because the hill's too steep and we couldn't get a tractor in there. That's something you have to consider when you plant grapes—can you maintain the row? Can you get the fruit out? I have to be able to hoist a thousand pounds of fruit with the tractor and you *don't* want to tip over in a loaded tractor. That's one reason we haven't planted the other side plot, the two acres down in the southeast corner, because there's such a big dip there that the thought of driving the tractor in there gives me the willies.

Jesse pulls out an aerial photograph of the vineyard, taken from a thousand feet up, and he shows me the house and the winery, and he circles the compost heap in the southwest corner of the estate, and he shows me the faint straight line that is the dusty road to the winery lined with curious ground squirrels and thistles and goldfinches, and he sketches out the rows and plots and blocks we have talked about, and shows me how he and his dad have carefully left two main east-west paths climbing the steep hill on either side of the big central plot, and how they left two smaller north-south paths open at the top of the hill (between the Wadenswil and the Bien Nacido) and the bottom (between the last chardonnay block and the Pinot Pierre)

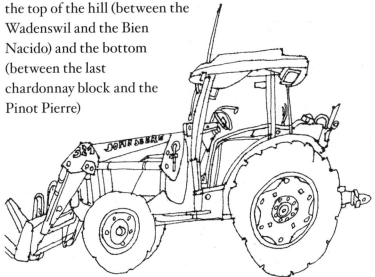

so that tractors and trucks have access everywhere, and I notice that the entire northeast corner of the estate, a chunk of land that looks to be about two acres in toto, is, according to the photograph, not only unplanted but densely forested.

How come that's not planted? I ask.

Waaay too steep, says Jesse. So steep that we built the fence right here, where it falls off sharply, though the property line is way over there at the edge of the photograph. That's a jungle down there. No one's been in there for years, I bet.

On the way home I find myself speculating about that particular piece of the Red Hills of Dundee, two acres of some of the finest pinot noir land in the world covered not with grapes but with fir and fern, oak and alder, elderberry and salmonberry, starflower and starwort, fringecup and buttercup, goatsbeard and nightshade, waxflower and candyflower, and bugleweed and smartweed, paintbrush and pinedrop, coltsfoot and deerfoot, horsetail and horsehair, freckle-pelt and tattered-rag and forking-bone and pixie-cup and lover's-moss, so called because it only grows on tree stumps and it forms a thick green pelt like the softest blanket imaginable for sinuous sylvan swooning.

For a moment I ponder what mysterious animals might be taking refuge in there also—marten and mink, fisher and fox—and then I daydream one last Yamhelas guy, the leathery last of his clan, the Ishi of the Red Hills, living like a shadow in the dappled jungle of those two lost acres, watching quietly from the fringe of the forest as the future covers him like a tide.

STARTING A VINEYARD

A PRIL. A FRIEND OF mine who makes pinot noir in the valley tells me how she got started doing such a crazy thing. Her dad was a wine geek and she grew up drinking bordeaux and burgundy, and her husband spent a year working in a kitchen in France and developing a taste for excellent wine, so they decided, for reasons that now seem eminently nonsensical, as she says, to start a vineyard in Oregon. This was in 1971. She and her husband paid eight hundred dollars an acre for eighteen acres of former plum orchard and planted pinot noir, chardonnay, and riesling cuttings that they bought in California and carried north in their car.

We rented a farmhouse nearby, she says. It was across the road from the biggest turkey farm around and the turkeys lined up by the fence every day to stare at me as I walked by with my baby. I never got used to that smell. They smell like hell. That's the most intense pungent smell there is. And there were gophers all around the house and mice in the house. Our cat liked to eat the gophers and leave their teeth and whiskers and intestines on the doormat as trophies or gifts or something.

We planted peas, chard, lettuce, cabbage, squash, zucchini, leeks, tomatoes, cucumbers, peppers, corn, beans, melons, and pumpkins. We bought an old orchard tractor and poles and wire that bean farmers sold us when they switched from pole beans to bush beans. We bought another old tractor that came disassembled in what looked to be a thousand parts and my husband spent all his spare time trying getting it to work and he spent two months on it and when he finally got it running it would turn only to the right, which sent us into hysterics.

We disked and tilled the land and then planted our vines six feet apart and ten feet between each row, which is not as wide apart as vineyards in California, but we felt like we were just going to see for ourselves what was right up here. That first year we planted two acres of pinot noir and two acres of reisling and an acre of chardonnay and then we waited. We raised walnuts and cherries and peaches and prunes while we were waiting for the vines to produce, which they did finally, and we sold our grapes from our first harvest to Dick Erath and David Lett, who made what we thought was pretty good wine from our fruit, so we realized it was time to think about making wine ourselves, which was nuts because we were trying to manage vineyards and orchards and two more babies, and we had no money, but we went for it anyway, and in 1977 we crushed forty-five tons of grapes and made three thousand cases of wine, which turned out to be excellent wine, especially the pinot noir. Now we make thirty thousand cases of wine a year, and it's better wine than it was thirty years ago too, and now I am the president of the company and two of our three children work here and there isn't a turkey for *miles* around, thank god.

She tells me this grinning as we wander through her vineyards, which stretch almost as far as the eye can see, ending at the foot of a ridge to the north.

This ridge is also covered with grapevines, planted noticeably wider apart, and I ask my friend what's the deal up there, and she says, smiling, that's France. That's the thirty-million-dollar hill, the place where France came to Oregon and everything changed.

She says this with a smile but her eyes are hard to read. What do you mean? I ask. That's Domain Drouhin. You should visit them yourself.

As we walk back to her winery she is quiet but then a bluebird zooms by and she lights up again and spends the next

twenty minutes explaining how she's built birdhouses all
through the vineyard for bluebirds, which are native and were
once abundant in the valley but now are increasingly rare
because sparrows and starlings pick on them and because the
dead trees they nest in are generally cut down now rather than
left to be condos for owls and woodpeckers and bluebirds, so
my friend built nine bluebird boxes, with entrance holes exactly
38 millimeters wide to allow for bluebird bodies but exclude for
example starlings, although swallows and flycatchers and
titmice and wrens will compete for the box, says my friend, but
we keep an eye on things and screen the tenants, and we built
the boxes so that they face southeast, out of the prevailing
winds, and we make the boxes tight enough to keep out snakes,
and we leave a little extra grass and vegetation near the boxes so
the birds can find bugs and berries, and every year there are a
couple more bluebirds in the vineyard, which is neat. They're
lovely creatures and they don't eat grapes, which is *very* neat.
And they were here on this land long before people were, so I
feel kind of responsible for arranging suitable housing.

THE OREGON/NEW ZEALAND THING

APRIL. JESSE AND I get to talking about Australian pinot noir and South African pinotage, which is a cousin of pinot noir, and I ask him about the time he spent eight months in New Zealand and his face lights up and he spends the next hour telling me about the climate, geology, and wine culture of the central Otago Valley of New Zealand, which is the southernmost wine region in the world and where the conditions for growing pinot noir are excellent but dicey, which makes for excellent wine and disaster in fairly even doses, he says, like last spring when the freeze came and the growers there lost more than half their crop, which was a terrible blow to the growers and a blow personally to me, because I was going to work the harvest there, and one of these years I *will* go work a harvest there, maybe next year, because I had a ball living there, and it's time for me to go back, and now I'm armed with six years of experience and a thousand years of sharper questions.

I was twenty years old when I was there, at Lincoln University in Canterbury, he continues. I was on an exchange program from Oregon State University, and there were two spots open in Canterbury, and I got one, in the viticultural and oenological program, and my friend Carson got the other, in forestry. Most of the folks I studied with there went into the wine business. There's Tim, he's funny as all get out, he's a Kiwi, he started a vineyard management company with Gary, who's Canadian, and there's Victoria, a Kiwi, who started her own export company, we dated for a month, and William, a Kiwi who ended up coming to Oregon and working at wineries and marrying a Kiwi he met here and now they live in California somewhere. The whole Oregon/New Zealand thing is really interesting, you know, you wouldn't be*lieve* how many young Kiwis come here to the valley to work for a while, and how many young Oregonians work down there. There are French folks here, and a few Australians, but the bulk of people from abroad coming to work in the wineries and vineyards in the valley are Kiwis, which is interesting to think about the subtle cultural effect, you know, people from an island in the south seas where the Maori were the first culture coming to work in a valley in the northern hemisphere where the Yamhelas were the first culture, you wonder at the interplay and intersection and all.

We all worked hard in Canterbury, he continues. We managed an eighth of an acre of chardonnay, sort of an experimental plot. I was penniless. Didn't even have a bicycle, let alone a car. I brought eight flyfishing rods with me from Oregon and sold them off one by one to get by. The dean of the university and I had a few meetings about unpaid bills although ultimately I did pay off every penny after I got home and started earning some money. I used to steal bread and those peanut-butter-and-jelly packets from the student union and fill my pockets with them. I ate a *lot* of peanut butter and jelly. Never been much for peanut butter and jelly since then, actually.

I remember everything, he says. I remember the vibrant colors, the shocking blue of the sky. I remember kiwi birds, and wild boar and deer in the forests, and koa parrots that liked to nibble on car tires and anything else rubber, and the smell of lamb pies in the shops, and the tiny cars, not like here. I remember tramping through the mountains looking for perfect rivers to fish. Rainbow trout and brown trout, both introduced to the rivers long ago by the British.

I remember that people there were so kind to me, he says. To not be in America at that age was huge. It was a huge education for me just to be out of Oregon, away from my family, out in the world, to realize that there was a vast world

out there that had nothing to do with everything I knew. That was an eye-opener.

I tell him of a remark by the wonderful Oregon writer Barry Lopez to the effect that the best thing educationally and spiritually for any young person is to leave town for a while and Jesse says yeh that's totally right, and the fact is that you really maybe don't appreciate your home place until you leave and can come back to it with new eyes.

There were some extraordinary moments in New Zealand, he continues. I remember touring the Seresin winery in Marlborough and tasting their pinot noirs and learning which clones they were using. I remember tasting sauvignon blancs and rieslings in Marlborough, those dry chalky grassy lemony stony wines that are famous now but then were just starting to be known outside New Zealand. I remember falling in love with a girl who was an Olympic field hockey player for New Zealand and one night with her sitting over the harbor sipping a wonderful riesling—a Giessen, as I remember.

Would you go back to New Zealand? I ask.

In two seconds, he says. Maybe one second.

What happened to the girl, the Olympic hockey player?

Time for me to get back to work, he says.

THE PEOPLE

PERHAPS THE MOST ATTENTIVE early historian of the
Yamhelas people who used to stroll across the Langes'
hillside, as they were beginning to be shoved off the land and
into history, was a minister and archaeologist named Robert
Summers, who lived with them for eight years, from 1873 to
1891. Summers is himself a riveting story: born in Kentucky,
schoolteacher in Hannibal, Missouri (where he may have been
the schoolteacher limned in Mark Twain's *Tom Sawyer*),
traveler across the plains to Oregon at age twenty-six, he
settled briefly near the Red Hills in 1855 before wandering on
again (selling his land, now under pinot noir vine, for eight
hundred dollars, eight cows, and eight pigs) as far as Europe
and Central America. At age forty-three, now married to a
musician and linguist named Lucia, and renowned for "his hair,
which was gray and hung in long curls to his shoulder," he
became the first Episcopal minister of Seattle, then a grubby
village of five hundred souls; two years later he and Lucia came
back to the Yamhill Valley, where he became the first
Episcopal priest at McMinnville, for a congregation of sixteen
families that met in a church two blocks from where Eyrie
Winery is today.

A curious and energetic soul, the Reverend Summers, who
had a sharp eye for the ways and manners and customs and
crafts of the Yamhelas or Cheamhill people, and his journal
tells us these things of the men and women and children who
had lived in the Red Hills for thousands of years: They loved to
dance and did so at the slightest excuse. Their funeral wakes
went on for days and days. When an earthquake spoke all the
men ran to their drums and drummed in response. Their
arrowheads, they told him, had been made in ancient times by

geese-men who chewed stone. They made beads from petrified wood. They flattened the heads of their children, considering the flattened forehead a sign of nobility and grace. They carved tiny canoes as cradles for their children and lined the cradles with moss and rabbit-skin. They made rattles from deer hooves and dice from beaver teeth. They considered paper to be a thing from sorcerers. They liked to build enormous fires. They built their houses from enormous cedar pillars and planks. Most women wore their hair in two long braids and wore earrings and nose-rings made of seashells traded from the coast. Men and women both wore necklaces made of elk teeth as amulets against bad luck. They liked to eat dried wild apples and dried wild pears and dried wild peas and dried wild salmon and dried blueberries and huckleberries and chokecherries and thimbleberries. They liked to eat roasted seeds of every sort. They liked bread made of wapato and camas tubers. They liked to eat bear and antelope and pheasant and ground squirrel. Most of all they liked to eat deer. They traded with tribes and clans and people from as far away as Alaska, Idaho, and California. The men of the People conducted an annual autumn holy festival during which they danced and sang all night and ate and slept all day for six days, rejoining their families and returning to work on the seventh day. Their priests were ordained by many days of fasting on a sacred mountain to the west. After ordination on the peak of the sacred mountain a priest could understand the languages of animals and could kill a person with a hard look. The price for killing someone accidentally with a hard look was four animals.

They called themselves Cheamhill, the People of the Stepping Stone River, after the place in the river where it could be forded at all seasons. Some of their words were *wamka*, the gopher, and *wapsutsi*, the mole, and *siaaah*, the shy blue grouse who lives in trees. Some of the People at this time were Ilkill, who was a very old man, and Kizad, who was his wife, and Chocote, who was a doctor and priest, and Kiarlpi, whose

mother taught her how to make extraordinary baskets, and
Sangasec, whose eating-spoon was made from the skull of an
elk, and Toyusah, who was very good at pounding camas root,
and Yatzkawah, who had a bad temper and was blind and once
drank seven bottles of whiskey in a day, and Poyusah, who was
a very good deer-hunter and once killed thirteen deer in a
week, and his wife Tatwani, who told the Reverend Summers
quietly that the People were having fewer children every year
and so were fading away, and Sulkia, who was also a very good
deer-hunter and never forgot to help the aged and feeble, and
Settesin, who was an orator and gave a speech in McMinnville
on the Fourth of July 1877 in which he said *We are men and not
dogs, and should not be driven hither and thither like cattle, not
having done anything to deserve such treatment,* which speech was
published in the newspaper a week later.

But Tatwani was right: the People had fewer children every
year, and by the time of the Second Great War the Cheamhill
culture had melted away. There are descendants of the People
in the valley still, living mostly on the Grand Ronde Reservation
to the west, near the holy mountain where once their priests
were given the languages of animals. Some five thousand men
and women and children live today on Grand Ronde, the descendants of many ancient Peoples: Calapooia, Molalla, Umpqua,
Clackamas, Tumwater, Shasta, Klickatat, Wasco, Paiute,
Klamath, Moatwa, Tekelma, Clatsop, Nestucca, Tillamook,
Nehalem. The primary source of income for the Confederated
Tribes of the Grand Ronde Community of Oregon, as they were
formally christened by President Ronald Reagan in 1983, is a
bustling casino along the road once used for trading seashells
from the coast. The casino is named for the holy mountain and
brings in enough money annually that the Confederated Tribes
of the Grand Ronde have established a charitable foundation
that makes grants to many educational and cultural entities
outside the reservation, almost all of them run by white people.

EBB & FLOW

A PRIL. I WANDER UP to the vineyard and the tasting
room is packed, people bellied up to the bar three rows
deep and not only Gabriel but Laura and Jesse pouring and
smiling and explaining and selling and chaffing and taking
names and orders and cash and credit cards, and I sit in the
corner and study Gabriel at work. He is the manager of the
tasting room and a cheerful exuberant quick-witted confident
ambitious eager young man with firm convictions about
people and wine based on many hours of considering and
contemplating people and wine. He spins and bends and
scribbles and answers the phone and pops corks and works the
credit-card machine (*whhaachungggg!*) and shakes hands and
makes change and wields wineglasses and pours two bottles at
once and grins and listens and twice sketches wee quick little
maps for visitors heading back down into the valley.

When the crush of visitors melts I ask him about people
and wine and the dynamics of the tasting room, and he says,
Well, my theory is that the weather dictates much of the ebb
and flow in the tasting room. Today is a good example. It's
overcast but not raining. It's the sort of day that people don't
really want to spend working in their yards, but it's relatively
warm, and so it's a good day to go adventuring, and we're sort
of an adventure up here, you have to come three miles off the
main road to get here, which is why we don't get the wine tours
and buses and vans that the bigger wineries along the highway
do. Which is good, because that means we don't get the heavy
drinkers, the people who go from winery to winery and get
hammered. Tour-hammered. Very rarely will I get someone
here who has too much to drink. The people who come up here

to taste our wines are basically self-selected. They make the
effort to be here. They're not coming up here just to drink
wine; they're coming for *our* wine. And for the winery, for the
experience. A lot of them are repeat visitors. More than half of
our visitors have been here before. Most first came on word of
mouth. Someone told them about the wine or the winery and
they're curious and they make us a destination. Or as Jesse says
they had a glass or a bottle in a restaurant and they're curious
about where and how it was made. My sense from talking to
our visitors is that many are also interested in local foods from
the valley, cheeses and nuts and wines and berries and such,
and in late summer especially we'll see a lot of people with
berry flats in their trunks, bags of hazelnuts, sacks of walnuts.
Which I tell them is a fine meal with pinot noir, a handful of
hazelnuts and blackberries and a glass of the estate.

I ask Gabriel about purchasing patterns and class
distinctions and the kinds of cars that visitors drive and the
kinds of clothes they wear and how much people spend per visit
and gender and age distinctions in consumption and purchase
and he lights up and says, Well, I've really thought about this.
Wine demographics are sort of the reverse of what you expect.
Rich people are basically cheap, and people who aren't rich—
people like, well, you—will generally buy more than rich people.
I think it's an impulse thing that has to do with the experience
of being here, the adventure, the way our bottle on your shelf
calls forth the memory of being up here. I've sold amazing
amounts of wine to non-wallets and amazingly tiny amounts of
wine to people with the most expensive cars. The clothes don't
much matter, I find. You can't gauge income from outerwear.

And, says Gabriel, we sell more wine on days when we
have fewer visitors. The quieter days are your better days.
There's more talking. More talking, more connection, more
sales. People want to connect. Wine is basically about

connecting. Which is why wine consumption is booming, I think. All kinds of people are buying more wine. Women are buying more wine. Young people are buying more wine. We get a lot of young couples here. Which again is part of us being a destination. It's romantic to come here. The whole experience of going to a winery up here in the hills and spending the afternoon sipping and talking is romantic.

Are you in the business because it's romantic? I ask.

O no, says Gabriel, grinning. No one who makes or sells wine finds it romantic at all after the first hour. Get Jesse going on this subject sometime if you want a laugh. Making wine is farming, and farming is hard. But the *product* of the farm is fascinating because ultimately wine is about people eating and talking and laughing and telling stories. Which is why I have the best job here. I like people and stories. I like gauging people as they walk in. It's a form of literature. I like making the shy people comfortable. I like giving them something they didn't have before and can't get quite in the same way at any other winery, an interesting experience, maybe some scrap of education about wine, of course, but you'd be surprised at the number of times that wine *isn't* the subject as they sip the wine. You'd be surprised at the directions some conversations take at this counter. I should write a book of the stories people tell *me*. Especially women. Sometimes I think I do my job best when I don't say anything at all. You have to train yourself to stop talking, you know. You have to train yourself to listen attentively. Which is sometimes what our visitors want even more than our wine.

IMAGINE WHAT THE TROUT
THINK OF THAT

O NE DAY I GET to talking to a friend who studies water flow and quality and retention and such in the valley and he tells me all sorts of things. He notes that just over half the valley is farmed, mostly for grass seed and the rest for orchards, berry fields, tree nurseries, vineyards, and hopfields. He tells me that the People who were here thousands of years ago deliberately set small fires every summer to keep the land open, mostly for berry bushes. He tells me that once the People were gone and the summer burns ceased the hills grew up remarkably thick in white oak and Douglas fir. He tells me that as far as archeologists can tell the most common groundcover when the People were around was a tall perennial grass called tufted hairgrass which didn't mind periodic fires and steady rain from November through June. That's one tough grass, he says, and there are still little patches of it here and there in the valley if you look for 'em, and the way to tell if it's tufted hairgrass or not is that it's waaay taller than you are. He tells me that at the present moment all streams and creeks and rivers in the valley are technically Overallocated for Water Rights, which means that seasonal demand exceeds supply, which means that more people want water for their crops than there *is* water if everyone called in their water chits, but at the present moment, he says, everyone *doesn't* exercise their full water rights, which is good, although someday soon everyone *will* exercise their water rights, which I predict will be a major problem. He tells me that as far as general water quality goes the streams and creeks and rivers in the valley are relatively clean but the main river they all end up heading toward, the mighty Willamette, is pretty much a mess, what with fecal coliform, mercury, fish deformities, high temperature, elevated pH, high nutrient levels, fouled sediments, and high amounts of trace metals. He tells me that the period of greatest concern for pollution or contaminant loading, as he says, of creeks and streams and rivers in the valley is from July through September, when pollutants like motor oil accumulate between infrequent rainfalls and are then washed into streams with relatively low rates of flow because of the lack of rain, for example, he says, like when it doesn't rain for five weeks, and a million cars and trucks and trailers and winnebagos and slipstreams rumble across the vast parking lots at the casino and then it rains hard one day and five weeks of oil and antifreeze and soda cans and cigarettes and tobacco spit sloshes into the creek, imagine what the trout think of *that*. He tells me that the most abundant native fish in the valley in the old days were cutthroat trout, which are still here but there's a lot fewer of them, he says, and there are some steelhead running in the creeks and rivers in winter, and there's some coho salmon which were brought back into the valley thirty years ago and they've done pretty well, but all in all it's your cutthroat who could make the best comeback, they're tough little dudes if they get clean cold water, and I can see a future where there's twice as many vineyards and wineries and twice as many cutthroat and people come to the valley from around the world to fish for trout and eat fresh native trout while sipping fresh native wine, I could see that. Or I could also see a hell of lot more parking lots and creeks full of oil and shopping carts and milk cartons and carp with three eyes and all. So when people say of the valley that We Are the New Napa I always think there's two ways to take that remark.

THE WINEMAKER'S BEST FRIEND

MAY. A CRISP WHIRLING day on the hill, swirls of wind dervishes, hawks sliding sideways suddenly, bursts of robins and juncos on intent secret headlong missions. A robin arrows by my ear at about ten thousand miles an hour and I mutter darkly about its mother being a wanton wicked hussy and Jesse grins.

We wander through the old block, Jesse pinching wee little new clusters of grapes as we go and dropping them casually on the ground.

Um . . . aren't those going to be precious pinot noir grapes that will be made into the holy grail? I ask, silently calculating how many gallons of excellent wine are being wasted by this insane youth in a most careless and reckless way.

You want two clusters to a cane, says Jesse, pinching away. We'll send the crew through here in a few days to trim. May is when vines really get to work—flowering, sending out shoots and suckers, leafing like mad, and you want to tell the vine where to go, train its energy, focus all that life, because otherwise they'd go nuts, they'd go wild with growth. They're sun junkies. It'd be a jungle in here if we didn't thin and trim regularly. What you want during flowering is a slight breeze moving among the rows all the time, ideally five to ten miles per hour, so they all get enough light and air and a chance to fertilize each other. And also we'll pull leaves on the east side of the rows more than the west, because the west side gets more sun and I don't want the fruit to get burned. You can taste the burn on fruit that got a little too much sun. Too much sun ruins the berries.

As I am scribbling this down I nearly topple into a plowed furrow the size of a small ditch, and I notice that there is a furrow neatly plowed down every row in the entire vineyard. I ask Jesse why, and he says, Because grasses and wildflowers suck water like you wouldn't believe, and we want the vines to get first crack at the water, so Chuy went through here yesterday with the tractor.

Where is he today?

Still on the tractor, says Jesse, but a different job, see? and he points to the bottom of the hill, where I see the little tractor grumbling along through the scrawny rows of new chardonnay vines, with Chuy astride and completely covered by a yellow protective suit and hood and mask.

Looks like he's from Pluto, I say.

He's a good guy, says Jesse. He never rests, not for a minute.

Why the suit?

He's spraying copper sulfate, says Jesse. New vines are really touchy and vulnerable and liable to all kinds of pests and diseases, and he's taking care of the babies. Sometimes we spray kelp extract on the new vines to give them a little healthy medicine.

We walk back uphill to the winery, me pondering how seaweed from the Oregon coast is absorbed by grapevines in the Oregon hills, which themselves are absorbed by Oregonians, who themselves are eventually absorbed back into Oregon sea or soil, and this all seems like a cool metaphor for something or other, but I don't have time to figure it out because now we are back in the winery, which today is a muddy mess of tools and tanks and tubs and such, and I ask Jesse casually about machines and equipment at a winery, which strikes such a sensitive chord in him that he sails off into a rant so long and heartfelt that recording it leaves me inkless and snorting with laughter.

The fact is, he says, his brow furrowing, that winemakers are all amateur mechanics, always fixing machines or *trying* to fix machines, and there are so *many* machines and so *much* equipment, my God, you wouldn't believe how much *stuff* you need to make wine, or *not* make wine because you are fixing *stuff*, I mean, really, it's bad *enough* that winemaking is really farming, which is really hard, but the secret to farming, besides working your ass off, is more equipment than Noah could fit on the freaking ark. I mean, really: tractor, cultivator, rototiller, mowers, sprayer, trucks, tanks, barrels, shovels, rakes, hoes, post-pounders, wire—my God, *miles* of wire, you wouldn't be*lieve* how much wire, I see it in my sleep . . .

Uh, Jesse . . .

My *God*, the huge spools of wire when Wally and I built the fence, I'll never forget
it, *there was so much
wire* . . .

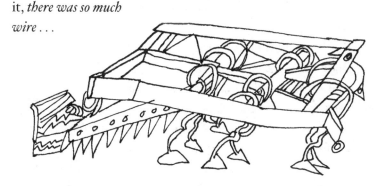

Jesse, the stuff, the equipment?

O, yeh, he says, posts, shears, machetes, tubing, stakes, corks, bottles, bottling machine, labeling machine, press, crusher, ladders, hammers, screwdrivers, brooms, mops, computers, telephones, generators, pipes, lightbulbs, test tubes, tongs . . . wire . . .

What's your favorite piece of equipment? I ask, trying to distract him from the whole wire thing.

Probably this, he says, picking up a long wooden tool that looks like a salad fork on steroids. This is what we use to push down the muck in the fermenter, the crushed grapes and skins and all. Some people use boat oars for this job.

What's this called?

Doesn't have a name.

Really? A tool with no name?

Which is why I like it, he says. Also I like that it *doesn't break down*. Yessir, the pusher-downer, the winemaker's best friend.

You're losing it, I say, grinning.

Man, you wouldn't *believe* how much wire there was, he says, the nightmare bursting out again. It was *awesome*. My hands still hurt. I don't go near the fence, you know, because it makes my hands hurt. Really. Don't laugh unless you too have wasted much of your precious youth building a wire fence eight feet tall.

But I cannot refrain from laughing, because he has the same look on his face that Wally has whenever I ask him about building the fence, which I do to tease him; a look of mingled amazement that the thing ever got done, and nasty male pleasure that some other poor muddy bastard had to do it too, and the awful memory of how much mulish male muscle had been expended, and relief at the realization, once again, that it's *done*, and doesn't have to be done again—not in *my* lifetime, anyway, says Jesse, beginning to smile again.

FRAGRANCE & GRAVITAS

MAY. I GET TO talking with a friend of mine in San
Francisco who knows more about wine than anyone I
know and we discuss the intricate intimate way that wine has
infused and enthused and enthralled human beings since before
recorded history, and he tells me, in his cheerful erudite way,
about how the Catholic miracle of the Eucharist comes directly
from a far more ancient belief that to eat bread and drink wine
was to eat the body of the corn god and drink the blood of the
vine god, and that Dionysus, child of a human mother and a
divine father, personifies the way wine comes from both earth
and sky and provides both nutrition and intoxication, and that
the grape vine for many thousands of years has been a powerful
symbol of persistent life because it flourishes in places that
seem too stark and stony for anything to live, and that wine for
many thousands of years was a basic foodstuff because people
desperately needed its six hundred calories per liter as energy
for the backbreaking mulish labor that was the fate of the
human species for untold thousands of years, and that wine for
thousands of years has been used as an antiseptic by physicians,
and that the primacy of wine as symbol in human culture can
be seen pretty much everywhere if you look closely enough—
the stylized wine cups we present as sports trophies, the
braided-vine motif in woven clothing and crests and logos and
heraldic shields, the ceremonial sparkling wine served at
moments of pressing joy or sadness, gate moments, moments
marking commencement of new lives or directions.

He is a remarkably learned man, my friend, educated by
sadness as well as books and universities, born under Nazi
bombs and residentially dichotomous all his life between
Europe and America, and every time I talk to him he tells me

ten things I didn't know, nine of which make me laugh and the
tenth of which breaks my heart, and our conversation this day
swings back, smiling, to religion and wine, because he is
intrigued that I am or was or will again someday be Catholic,
which he is not, and he tells me about the wines of the hill of
the popes in France, where the papacy was headquartered for a
while, and where the wines still are, as he says, richly colored,
sumptuous, and authoritative, as you would expect of wines
with papal associations, and where the vines grow in what
appears to be not so much soil as a jumble of tawny stones and
pebbles, where nothing else except thyme and lavender and
olives grow from deep clay and limestone, and where the dry
north wind blows for days on end, the legendary *mistral* roaring
down the Rhône valley, and all this, the stony soil and the dry
wind and the glaring Mediterranean sun, makes for intense
and elegant wines, as he says, wines with bravura, wines with
heady voluptuousness, wines of both fragrance and gravitas,
wines that were elixirs for prolonging youth and even life itself,
as one (long-lived) winemaker there said a century ago.

Good heavens, says my friend at last. All this talk has
given me a powerful thirst. I am going down cellar to pull a
Châteauneuf-du-Pape for dinner. I do wish that you and your
lovely wife were here. We would have almonds and lamb,
perhaps. Well, next time you are in the City we will choose
from among Château de Beaucastel, Château La Nerthe, or
Domaine du Vieux Télégraphe—perhaps the vintages of 1988
or 1989, which were superb. And you will see what I mean
about their intense elegance and bravura. *Au revoir, mon ami!*

I hang up the phone and walk straight to the wine shop
and get a bottle of Château La Nerthe and make lamb risotto
for dinner and when my lovely wife says *um, what's the occasion?*
I tell her it's a religious thing, hard to explain, and somehow
she understands.

CEDAR & MINT

MAY. I WANDER UP to the vineyard and ask Jesse about the taste and heft and flavor and characteristics and virtues and vices and essences and motifs and aromas and bouquets and noses and such of pinot noir, and he says, Well, there are many ways to talk about this, and many ways to make pinot, and pinot keeps changing as it ages. But there are some general principles. A young pinot noir just bottled will generally be a little fruity, with hints of cherry, raspberry, strawberry, blackberry, plum, currant. My dad says that a new pinot from our hill tastes like the black raspberries that were grown here. But a well-made pinot will deepen as it ages, and reveal darker flavors, thicker flavors—chocolate, smoke, truffles, almonds, tobacco, tea, leather, cedar, roses, mushrooms, licorice, mint.

Cedar? I ask. Mint? Is this the marketing copywriter talking to me?

It's hard to explain, he says, grinning, and you get silly awful quick. But this is why pinot noir is the most complex wine of all. If you have great grapes and handle them well you can make amazing wines. A fine pinot is balanced and structured and complex, with lots of sensual layers. And the scents and flavors change with time, which is fascinating. A bottle one year is a different bottle five years down the road or ten or twenty, which is cool.

Jesse gives me the speech again about how a really fine pinot noir needs to be beautifully balanced weightwise between a bright clean simplicity and a sinewy heft, which I disagree with utterly, being a big fan of sinewy heft, of sturdy dense muscular bold forceful pinot noirs, pinots with some major hair on them, not the prissy transparent pink pinots

that I drank first (and loved) when I first started drinking
pinots, but, as I tell Jesse, when I was a child I spake as a child,
I understood as a child, I drank the pinots of a child, but when
I became a man I put away childish things and developed a
yen for pinots with power and passion, light-heavyweights,
pinots that are Archie Moore and Billy Conn and Gene Tunney.

Huh? says Jesse.

Pinots that are Roy Jones Junior, I say, realizing again
that he is in his twenties and I am Methusaleh.

No no no, he says. The best pinot is a Marvin Hagler.
Strong but balanced, muscular but quick on its feet.

This line of talk sets me to ruminating the rest of the day,
and remembering the snowy night a thousand years ago when I
my own personal self saw a middleweight world title fight
starring the inimitable Marvelous Marvin Hagler, the greatest
middleweight there ever was, despite his eventual controversial
loss to the oily public relations master Sugar Ray Leonard, and
the memory of Leonard, the photogenic Olympic hero and
ubiquitous pitchman, not actually *defeating* the glowering
glaring Hagler but merely outshining him, impressing the fight
judges that night but by no stretch of the imagination
impressing Hagler or most of the crowd, sets my teeth on edge,
for there was something slippery and oleaginous and
untrustworthy and showy and flashy and phony and fake and
fulsome about Leonard, unlike Hagler, who was direct and
straightforward and honest and blunt and powerful and quiet
and had created himself miraculously and grimly after
surviving a childhood from the nether circles of hell.

With dinner that night I choose a pinot that turns out to
be, to my regret, a Sugar Ray Leonard—undeniably
accomplished, flashes of stunning grace and power, but
somehow less than it appears to be; more sales than substance,
as it were. I mention this to my wife, and explain my theory

about boxers as excellent metaphors for discussing the relative strength and quality of pinot noir, and explain how Jesse has it all wrong as to how muscular a pinot noir should be, and she gazes at me with a look that I cannot adequately explain, and says finally, But Jesse has made many thousands of bottles of wine, and you have made exactly zero, so why is it that I should be listening to you rather than the guy who actually makes the wine? Why is that?

A question I cannot answer, and not the first time she has rendered me speechless.

Some days later, thinking about the flavors of pinot noir, and grinning at the memory of Jesse saying the words cherry, plum, raspberry, strawberry, chocolate, smoke, truffles, almonds, cedar, roses, licorice, and mint, I spend some time happily collecting other words that people use to describe pinot noir: elegant, velvety, earthy, musty, pungent, fragrant, brilliant, glistening, shimmering, sparkling, aromatic, mysterious, discreet, harmonious, honest, clean, refined, ethereal, romantic, urbane, charming, sophisticated, graceful, debonair, silky, seamless, harmonious, intense, compelling, temperamental, sensitive, acerbic, pouting, strutting, spicy, sensual, succulent, supple, fleshy, lush, romantic, voluptuous, seductive, and I have to stop.

WINE YOU COULD CUT WITH A KNIFE

MAY. A FRIEND OF mine who is devout and Jewish and a scholar and a wonderful essayist sends me an essay of his about the four cups of wine that must be downed ritually at Passover Seders, which wine, he notes, is so heavy and sweet that it could fairly be mistaken for alcohol-fortified pancake syrup. This burly potation, he explains, is frequently assumed to be the quintessential kosher wine, the very thing Solomon quaffed after a long day of wisdom-making, but in fact the basic requirements for kosher wine are silent on the matter of taste, color, and texture, which has led to a sorry state of affairs in which the common American kosher wine is made from a New World grape, the Concord, that was promoted in the 1860s as a nativist retort to European vines believed to have been corrupted by their ancient "Semitic" (read: Jewish) origins.

This peculiar idea was the brainchild of Ephraim Wales Bull, a Concord goldleaf artisan and amateur farmer, who devoted himself to developing varieties of *Vitis labrusca,* the then-dominant North American grape species that would replace the morally degenerate European species, *Vitis vinifera,* as the source of American wine. The problem he faced, notes my friend dryly, was that *labrusca,* while hardier than *vinifera,* bore fruit that was a natural disaster: small, leathery-skinned, sour, and rank. Wine from it could most charitably be called harsh (other good words are *horrendous* and *swill*), but the Concord grape was being planted as far west as Missouri by 1865, when Horace Greeley called it America's "best grape for general cultivation."

A New Jersey dentist named Thomas Welch (who believed that his Savior had been a teetotaler and that New

Testament citations of wine were therefore references to a non-alcoholic grape drink) added copious amounts of sugar to the juice to make Doctor Welch's Church Wine in 1869. His son Charles changed this muck to Welch's Grape Juice in 1893, the first American beverage to promise male drinkers sexual advantage ("The lips that touch Welch's are all that touch mine"). The Concord grape went kosher in 1899 when a Polish immigrant named Sam Schapiro founded America's first kosher wine operation in a cellar on the Lower East Side of Manhattan, boasting that he made "wine so thick you can cut it with a knife." Today, while a few wineries experiment with kosher wine made from cabernet and merlot and pinot gris and pinot noir grapes, Schapiro's Kosher Winery and its competitors earn $27 million annually in sales of wine so thick you can cut it with a knife.

L'chayim!, my friend says, cheerfully.

DRINKING WINE WITH YER MATES

M AY. A FRIEND IN Australia tells me that it's almost
time for harvest there and he is taking a few minutes to
contemplate the long view of recent trends in the Australian
wine industry and to make me jealous of the wines he is
sipping and I am not, because, as he says, he's in the bonza
hemisphere and I am not.

I point out that he is technically in what is tomorrow for
me, so that I have a whole extra day in which to sip the superb
wines of the Red Hills of Dundee, and he says ah yes, but here
in Melbourne it's clear and dry and what you would call eighty
degrees, and there I bet yer wet, poor lad.

He notes that in the past fourteen years more than four
hundred wineries opened in his state alone, Victoria,
although, he says, I think some of those will fall by the
wayside after their owners realize what's really involved in
making wine. You imagine you can work in the city all week
as a banker or broker or whatever and then motor out to the
vineyard on the weekend and look at the vines looking after
themselves and sit on the porch drinking wine with your
mates from the city, but it's not like that at all. It's about
working seven days a week for five years without a break
before you ever get started. At least as far as I can tell.

He continues along this vein and then we get to talking
about how vineyards and wineries are excellent economic
boosters for rural areas because they not only employ
residents but also bring in lots of tourists who stay in hotels
and bed-and-breakfasts and patronize restaurants and cafes,
but he also notes that generally vineyard work is low-paid, so
that really what's happening, he says, is that more people are

working for lower wages, which is good, because more people are working in rural areas where populations otherwise have a general tendency to drain toward cities looking for employment, but it's not as good as it looks, because those people are not generally making enough of a living to save any money or contribute all that much to the local tax base.

My friend ends by chanting the names of the wine regions in his state, to make me grin and remember the crisp afternoons we had sipping wines by the sea, and the words gleam in my mind with the startling light of that country: Geelong and Goulburn, Henty and Heathcote, Bendigo and Beechworth, Sunbury and Strathbogie, Mornington and Murray and Macedon, the Pyrenees and the Grampians, Swan Hill, the Yarra Valley . . .

BOTTLED POETRY

M AY. I WANDER UP to the winery and get totally absorbed by the packaging of wine, the corks and bottles and labels and boxes in which the bottles are shipped and pallets on which the boxes to be shipped are shipped, and Jesse points out that even the words used to describe the bottling of wine are entertaining: a standard bottle of wine contains 750 milliliters, or 25 ounces, of wine, which is four-fifths of a quart, and a split is a quarter of a standard bottle, a magnum contains two bottles, a jeroboam contains four bottles, a rehoboam holds six bottles, a methuselah holds eight, a salmanazar holds twelve, a balthazar holds sixteen, and the imperial nebuchadnezzar contains within its vast glassy person twenty bottles of wine.

This reminds me irresistibly of the vast King of Hawaii, Kalakaua, the "Merrie Monarch," an enormous man who spent an afternoon in 1889 drinking pinot noir with a friend, the friend thin as a willow and cheerful as a swallow and a fan of the fermented grape since he was a child in Scotland raiding his playmate's lunch-box for raisin wine, and I tell Jesse what the skinny Scot wrote in a letter to a friend back home, "His Majesty is a very fine, intelligent fellow, but O, Charles! what a crop for the drink! He carries it too like a mountain with a sparrow on its shoulders. We calculated five bottles . . . in three hours and a half, and the sovereign was quite presentable, although perceptively more dignified at the end."

I get to telling Jesse stories about this willowy wit, my favorite writer there ever was, Robert Louis Stevenson, and how his most famous remark about wine, *wine is bottled poetry*, is actually printed in huge letters on massive signs at the north and south ends of Napa Valley, where he and his wife Fanny spent their honeymoon touring vineyards in the summer of

1880, and how he had casks of pinot noir shipped to him in his final years in Samoa, and how he once canoed through France stopping at every sizeable village for a glass of wine, probably many of those glasses pinot noir, and how he was famous among his friends for sitting at table over good wine for hours talking and laughing and telling stories, and how his friend Sidney Colvin said after he died that the world would mourn the loss of a genius artist but Stevenson's friends would mourn more the loss of a great table companion, and how Stevenson once hiked through the mountains of France with a donkey, stopping at every sizeable village for a glass of wine, probably many of those glasses pinot noir, and how he especially loved wines from the high vineyards of northern Italy, *those notable Valtellines that once shone upon the board of Caesar* as he wrote, and how all of his books have wine in them, from *A Child's Garden of Verses*, where he writes that every house should have a bin of wine, to *Jeykll and Hyde*, where the lawyer Mister Utterson has a "taste for vintages," to *The Black Arrow*, where Sir Daniel is in such turmoil of spirit that he cannot even drink his wine (!), and even to *Treasure Island*, when intrepid young Jim Hawkins is sent below-decks for a bottle by a conniving pirate and Jim asks politely, as any sensible civilized soul would, *Will you have white or red?*, and the foul scummy pirate replies, *Well, I reckon it's about the blessed same to me, shipmate, so it's strong, and plenty of it*, which reveals the man to be a rogue and dog and barbarian, and by now I am off and running on one of my favorite subjects, because I really and truly do think Stevenson is the greatest writer who ever wrote in English, the guy wrote first-class top-notch top-shelf brilliant vivacious energetic piercing stories in every genre except plays, there I have to confess he was a rotten playwright, but every other genre he had totally in hand, novels and essays and articles and history and biography and poems and prayers and letters and travel and even horror stories for heavenssakes, I mean, really, his book *The Merry Men* is scarier than any two modern horrortomes you can name, and Stevenson could turn even a *journal* into a really interesting book, which is what he did with his honeymoon in Napa, and talking about Napa brings me circling back to speculating about his taste for pinot noir, and remembering that he and Fanny tasted eighteen wines one day at a winery in Calistoga, and I try to remember the exquisite prose he wrote about wine in his honeymoon journal, *The Silverado Squatters*, but my memory for long prose passages is less than zero, and I get sidetracked anyway telling Jesse about Stevenson's poignant last hours in Samoa, and how he was helping his wife make a salad for dinner, and because she looked so tired and blue he went to the cellar and brought up the best bottle of Burgundy in the house, which he had just opened when he had the stroke that killed him, so he died with an open bottle of pinot noir on the table, and he was only forty-four years old, by all accounts a man of wonderful kindness and generosity of spirit, funny and fervent, a genius artist but perhaps even greater as a man, a man greater of heart than art, which is a goal I strive for and have never yet arrived at though I am trying as hard as I can most days.

Huh, says Jesse, I didn't know all that.

Later when I get home I riffle though *The Silverado Squatters* and find the passage I remembered and it is as sunny and cheerful and personable as its author: "The stirring sunlight, and the growing vines, and the vats and bottles in the cavern, made a pleasant music for the mind . . . Here earth's cream was being skimmed and garnered: and the customers can taste, such as it is, the tang of the earth in this green valley. So local, so quintessential is a wine, that it seems the very birds in the verandah might communicate a flavor, and that romantic cellar influence the bottle next to be uncorked . . . for a bottle of good wine, like a good act, shines ever in retrospect."

WHAT DID CHRIST DRINK?

JUNE. I SAY TO my erudite oenophiliac friend in San
Francisco, what wines would have been in those big jars at
the wedding in Cana, and what wines would have been near
Christ's elbow at the Last Supper?

A difficult question to answer, he says. But if we put
together what we know about wine in the ancient world, and
about some wine practices in those areas today, we might
conclude that it was common to allow the grapes to dry slightly
before they were crushed and fermented, raising the potential
alcohol to a level that would help prevent spoilage, concentrate
the acidity so the pH would be lowered and prevent bacterial
activity, and probably leave some residual sugar, always
welcome in the ancient world—caloric content, you know, for
the energy needed for constant physical labor. The ancients,
you will remember, did not have alcohol to fortify their
wines—the Arabs invented distillation much later—and
keeping wines wholesome once a jar was opened must have
been a problem.

Let me further speculate, said my friend, that whatever
was happening in Phoenicia, where winemaking skill
originated, was also happening in Crete, where wines have
been produced since time immemorial, and I have studied the
story of wine in Crete with some attentiveness. The reputation
of Cretan wine in imperial Rome was as great as it had been in
classical Greece five centuries earlier, and at least a thousand
years before that the Minoans had produced wine in the same
areas. The wine called Malmsey, for example, which made
Venice rich and England happy, probably resembled, at the
very least, similar wines produced on Crete—a dark smoky
amber wine, redolent and relatively sweet. Remember that

Homer's descriptions of wine are almost always qualified by words and phrases suggesting honeyed sweetness. His descriptions of wines are at least consistent with his account of grapes left in the sun to dry before pressing. And that seemed still to have been the practice when we again become aware of Cretan wine at the start of the thirteenth century, when, as her share of the spoils of Byzantium, Venice grabbed Crete.

So what Christ would have sipped was sweet? I ask.

Quite likely.

This makes me ponder that mysterious and paradoxical young Jewish man, and think about him for the thousandth time not as god but as a guy, traveling and eating and drinking with his friends, and telling stories, always telling stories. I note to my erudite friend that Christ was very familiar indeed with grapevines and fruit, and that he often used vines and wines as metaphors in his stories, and that he actually did of course once *make* wine, anywhere from 120 to 130 gallons at Cana ("six stone waterpots . . . containing twenty or thirty gallons each," notes John in his gospel, one of the rare moments when the poetic Beloved Apostle attends to factual detail), and that Christ's wine was ranked as "good" by the startled headwaiter, but that the Christos—real name, Yesuah ben Joseph—is not recorded as actually *drinking* wine anywhere in the gospels, except for the sponge full of sour wine forced into his mouth as he died, but that he must have sipped and savored many a wine in his day, because he says at the Last Supper that he will not drink of the fruit of the vine again until he can drink it new with his companions at the coming of the kingdom of God, a remark I always found hauntingly sad.

That night with dinner I open a fruitful bottle of shiraz, and silently dedicate the first sip to the young man who died long ago believing that love would defeat murder, life defeat death, hope defeat despair. How wrong he was, considering all the evidence since—but how right I hope him to be. *L'chayim.*

A ONE-WINERY DOG

JUNE. THE ANNUAL SPRING Release Party at Lange, for people on the mailing list and various and sundry other friends of the winery, is set for what is for weeks forecast to be the sunniest driest weekend of the year, so of course on both days it rains oceans and ocelots. It rains so hard Sunday that the burble of conversation in the winery as people taste the new releases is nearly drowned by the hammering of rain on the roof, and people with glasses in their hands poke their heads out the side door to see if there are trout in the trees yet or what.

Jesse and Gabe are opening six wines, two whites and four pinot noirs. The guests—maybe a couple hundred, all told, spread out from noon to four—start with the whites and then finish with the reds. The whites are the new pinot blanc—last fall's grapes, fermented for seven months in a stainless steel tank—and the new reserve chardonnay, grapes from two years ago, fermented for sixteen months in tank and barrel. The pinot noirs are all from grapes grown two years ago and aged in barrels for sixteen months: the Reserve (Don and Jesse's favorites from the barrel room, blended to make what Jesse calls chef's choice), the Three Hills Cuvee (grapes from Lange's vineyard, Wally's vineyard, and the Freedom Hill vineyard, blended to make an annual vintage that annually makes me moan with joy), and the single-vineyard pinots from Freedom Hill (Dan and Hellen Dusschee's vineyard, twelve miles south) and Cancilla (Ken Cancilla's vineyard, on the west wall of the valley).

There's also a table of catered snacks—tiny mushroom tarts, prosciutto and melon bruschetta, diced fruit, sliced baguette—and the guests wander around sipping and chatting and asking questions and dangling babies and wolfing tarts and snorting bouquet and finally exiting through the door to the tasting room, where most of them, I notice, buy a case of wine on their way back to their cars.

I wander around the room listening. Some people, generally male, ask winehead questions—brix levels of the grapes, blending percentages in barrel. Other people, generally female, remark the wine itself, its bouquet, its feel in the mouth. People of both genders are curious about provenance—vineyard sites, elevation, soils. People of both genders make a point of congratulating the winemakers. A number of people say nothing whatsoever and just sip the wines, smiling. I notice five infants in four hours, all of them patient and silent and attentive amid the bustle. I watch one boy, perhaps five years old, quietly station himself by the snack table and efficiently mow down an entire platter of pineapple chunks. I watch one older man make three rounds of the wines, eighteen sips in all. I watch Gabe and Jesse infinitesimally shrink the amount of wine they pour per tasting as the afternoon wears on. I watch the cheerful woman who provides the snacks replenish her entire table four times, five times in the case of the pineapple chunks. I watch people, generally men, scribble notes on their tasting sheets. I watch the rain. I watch my subtle research assistant as she falls into intimate conversations with people, generally female, with the greatest of unselfconscious ease. I watch a dog the size of a small pony sniff curiously at the vast barrels of pinot gris stacked to the ceiling behind us. His human being tells him to Stay! and the dog sits down companionably next to me and we regard each other politely and I offer him a sniff of the new Freedom Hill pinot noir, the wine from twelve miles away, but he declines.

Not much for pinot noir, eh? I remark to his owner.

He doesn't like wine, says his owner. He likes beer, but only in summer. And he's discriminating, too. He won't drink regular beer. He only likes microbrew. I suppose I shouldn't be giving him beer at all, I'm sure it's not good for him, it's probably illegal or something, but on a really hot day, late in the afternoon, when I am having an ale on the deck, I pour him a little in a bowl, and you should see his face. You never saw a happier dog in your life. It's like a commercial for microbrew ale.

Do you bring him to tastings a lot?

Only here, says his owner. He likes coming up here. I brought him to a tasting once at another winery and he wouldn't even walk through the door. Balked at even entering the place. He's a one-winery dog.

Customer loyalty is a great thing, I say.

Yeh, says the owner. I should tell Don. That'd make him smile.

PINOKANAGAN

ONE DAY I CASUALLY start paging through a book big enough to stop traffic, and soon find myself utterly absorbed, for the book is John Winthrop Haeger's magisterial *North American Pinot Noir*, which turns out to be (a) the bible of the poet's grape in America and (b) a pleasure to read. All wine commentary, like all poetry, is liable to blather and fluff, stuff and nonsense, hooey and wind, but Haeger is one of those rare souls who brings together the science of growing the grapes with the craft of making the wine with the history of who made it and how and straight talk about what it tastes like and why.

Plus he's a sucker for facts, and facts are our friends. Some pinot facts: There are twenty-seven thousand acres of pinot noir planted in North America—about the acreage of Manhattan. Those acres are only 6 percent of all the red wine grapes planted on the continent. Some 90 percent of these pinot noir grapes are planted on the Pacific coast between the Columbia River and the Santa Barbara Channel. Of the other 10 percent of pinot in the U.S. and Canada, there are some surprising locations: in Canada, there are pinot vineyards on the shore of Lake Ontario and in the Okanagan Valley of British Columbia; in the States there are pinot plots in Ohio and Arizona, among other states. Pinot noir grows where John Steinbeck and Jack London and Jack Kerouac and M.F.K. Fisher and Julia Child and Ken Kesey and Beverly Cleary lived. Pinot noir may have been made at Carneros as early as the 1840s by the son-in-law of Mexican commander Mariano Vallejo, who used "a soft cow hide and strong-legged Indians" to crush his grapes. Vines from Peru were planted by Russian settlers on the coast of Sonoma County where now pinot rules. Joseph Swan, a pinot pioneer in the Russian River Valley of California, was the son of teetotalers in North Dakota, but he grew fascinated by wine as a child and made his first wine from rhubarb, crushed through the wringer of his mom's washing machine and fermented in a crock hidden in the attic. Dick Ponzi, a pinot pioneer in Oregon, was an aeronautical engineer who designed rides at Disneyland. Rodney Strong, a pinot pioneer in Sonoma County, had been a professional ballet dancer in Germany. Richard Sanford, in whose vineyard Don Lange worked his first harvest, was so shattered by his experiences as a soldier in Vietnam that all he wanted to do with the rest of his life was work with living things born from holy dirt. The first wines in the Okanagan Valley in British Columbia were made from apples. The first pinot vines there covered a fifth of an acre—about the size of a football field. The first vineyard by Lake Ontario was planted in the rectory garden of an Episcopal church. There are pinot noir vineyards near the town of Dundee, New York. The highest pinot noir vineyards in North America are probably those in the Jemez Mountains of New Mexico, more than a mile above sea level.

North Carolina has 1.5 acres of pinot noir in the entire state. Pinot grows in areas that receive 40 inches of rain a year and in areas that receive 15 inches of rain a year. Critics of some California pinots have accused them of tasting like silage. One favored clone of the many pinot clones planted in North America is named for the estate of the commander of the Swiss army in the First World War. A clone suspected of having been smuggled into North America without the proper flurry and folderol of permissions and permits is called a suitcase or Samsonite clone. Grapes picked at less than 23 degrees brix (sugar level) produce a wine with less than 12.5 percent alcohol; grapes picked with brix levels above 26 make wines with more than 14.4 percent alcohol. The whole time between the moment when grapes are sludged into the fermenter until the new wine is pressed out of the redolent sludge wears one word: vatting (in French, *cuvaison*). The French use a tool called the *pige* to push the muddle of skins and seeds and stems back down into the fermenting juice of the grapes. When pinot noir was reborn in America in the 1960s it was mostly racked not in oak casks but in tanks made of redwood.

Even the calm and urbane Haeger finally throws up his hands when trying to explain the poet's grape, however. "Pinot is inexplicably moody," he writes. "A lot of sweat and tears were shed to get pinot making to where it is today [in North America]," but "even today there are many easier ways of making a living."

THE DEVIL MADE PINOT NOIR

JUNE. I SAY TO Jesse one day, c'mon, how hard *is* it really to grow pinot noir? I mean everyone I talk to is always pissing and moaning about how hard it is to grow it, and how it's like a wheezing genius hothouse orchid that has to be coddled and nursed like a fading movie star, and I expect him to grin like he usually does but he only half grins and the other half is wince, and it turns out that he's had a looong day in the vineyard worrying about his grapes, because off he sails on a monologue that begins by lauding the complexity and subtlety and nuance of the *wine* that comes from the grape, but then swerves into how the *grapes* are as thin-skinned as teenagers in a new school, and how the vines are all prissy about how they need *just* the right amount of sunlight and water, not *too* much, and not *too* little, and how they totally quail and fail under rain that falls too *hard*, and they swoon at the *slightest* stress, and you have to darn well nearly feed them with a *spoon* when they're babies, and you might as well go around the vineyard at night and swaddle each vine in a *blanket* for heavenssake, and rock them gently to sleep, and if a pinot noir vine even *suspects* there might be a virus on the same freaking *continent* it's ready to call it cancer or a brain tumor and give up the ghost, and it's pretty much like they spend all their time huddled moaning by the fireplace, asking you plaintively to go get them hot herb tea and a lozenge and a lurid novel, and sometimes you want to stand at the top of the hill and shout *get a grip!*

Uh—are you okay? I ask.

Yeh, he says, recovering his usual equilibrium. It's just that the vines are at kind of a crucial stage, and pinot noir can be, what's a polite word—fussy.

Later in my reading I come across other growers' dark references to pinot noir, which make me grin: *a minx of a vine that leads growers on a terrible dance,* and *moody and enigmatic and capricious,* and *petulant and tantalizing and quixotic,* and *the heartbreak grape,* and *cursed with a personality so sour it would make the grinch look like Santa Claus,* and *God made cabernet sauvignon, whereas the devil made pinot noir,* a remark attributed to the legendary early-California grower Andre Tchelistcheff, which when I report that line happily to Jesse he says yeh, well, but he was growing the vine in *California,* so there you are. All due respect to California.

KATOOMBA

UNE. A YOUNG AUSTRALIAN friend of mine says,
Remember sitting on the quay in Sydney by the Opera House
drinking that pinot noir? That was lovely wine, wasn't it? I've
tried to remember what exactly that wine was but for the life of
me I cannot remember. Stony Hill? Stony Bay? Stonier? I even
stopped by the café for their wine list so I could track it down
but they said their wine list had changed twice since we were
there that night and none of the pinots they have now is the one.

I tell him that I do indeed remember that bottle, and the
conversation that flew and flowed and wove and braided around
it as we sat at a little table and watched the fireworks light up
the gleaming dark harbor, because most of the riveting conversation that night was from the third member of our party, a
dapper older gentleman who had been born in Brisbane before
the war, when Brisbane was a sleepy dusty obscure little
Australian town, as he told us, until the Allies decided to make
it the nerve center for the war in the Pacific, and then, almost
magically, just like that, seemingly overnight, Brisbane became
rather an American city, he said, something along the lines of a
small Chicago, perhaps. But I remember the small town of my
childhood, he said, which of course is gone now except in memory,
and despite sensible acknowledgment of the inevitable entropy
and dissolution of things, one must rue the fact that ultimately the
passing of my generation will also mean the passing, in a real sense,
of the essentially rural Brisbane I knew as a child. Such is life.

I offer a toast to the city that once was, he said, and we all
sipped.

Our conversation that warm night on the quay swirled in
many directions, for my young friend is a naturalist and deft

storyteller, and the dapper older gentleman is a scholar and masterful storyteller, and I was and am utterly absorbed by stories and the way people tell them, and how stories weave and flow and braid, especially when there is good wine on the table, and that night there was excellent wine on the table, first a bottle of chardonnay, a crisp clean forthright wine from the Margaret River in western Australia, a friendly wine to sip as stories began, and then with dinner there was a terrific pinot noir from the Mornington Peninsula in southeastern Australia, a more substantive and denser wine as the stories opened and deepened, my young friend telling us of the waters he loves in the mountains of New South Wales, the rivers Kedumba and Nattai and Wollondilly and Burragorang and Wingecarribee and Megalong and Kanimbla, and of the plants he loves there, isopogon and leptospermum and xanthorrhoea and hardenbergia, and of the birds he loves, honeyeaters and whipbirds and spinebills and thornbills and rosellas, and of the way the country he loves burned two years ago, smoke everywhere like an omen, as he said, the air sodden with smoke, the moon tarnished, the nights smelling of apprehension, of remorse, of penitence, of sorrow.

I prayed water words all day and night, he said, I chanted an ancient Gundungurra word for falling water, *katoomba, katoomba, katoomba* . . .

As my young friend sang water words the dapper older gentleman and I sipped the darker denser wine, and the older gentleman loosened his tie and told more stories of the Brisbane he had known more than sixty years ago, stories of how his family had come to Australia from Lebanon in the 1880s and settled in what was at the time a sleepy dusty obscure little Queensland town, and how his grandfather held court at the café all day, drinking endless tiny cups of intense dense coffee and telling stories and adjudicating disputes and

wrangles among the Lebanese diaspora, and how his father's
family was so aghast that he was marrying a woman outside
their Catholic faith that not one of the family showed up at
the wedding, and he told stories of his ancient papery aunts
and the way they sat talking with their friends on verandas,
their thin voices whispering shards of stories among walls as
thin as paper, and of the vast parades of red gum trees that
once marched along the labyrinthine Brisbane River, and of
the immense fig and mango trees that cupped his weather-
board house like a toy in their huge green hands, and of the
possums and flying foxes that sailed through the trees, and of
the little streets in the city named for women, Alice and
Margaret and Mary and Charlotte and Elizabeth, and the
longer streets named for men, Edward and Albert and Henry
and Barry and Isaac, and my young friend and I sat absorbed
and riveted, sipping the dark wine, as Brisbane grew before
our eyes from a dusty former penal colony to a bustling rail
center for local produce, and then came the war, and rafts of
American and British and Scottish and Canadian soldiers and
Japanese prisoners, and the dapper gentleman left Brisbane
Grammar School for the University of Queensland, and then
set off on a lifetime of stories, the collecting and telling of
which had carried him around the world and finally back to
his native land, to the vast bustling sprawl of Sydney, the Big
Smoke as he called it, and to our little table by the glittering
harbor, where he finished his stories as we finished the bottle,
and he reknotted his tie just so, and bowed, and took his leave,
walking briskly away down the quay, the long-ago city of his
boyhood still fresh in his heart. My young friend and I sat at
the table quietly for a few minutes, sipping coffee, staring at
the harbor, feeling very much that we were still in Brisbane, a
long time ago, before the war.

A SUBTLE SCENT

JUNE. GRAPEVINE-FLOWERS. I wander up to the winery
and wander through the old pinot noir block and discover
that once again Jesse is right, this time about the incredibly
tiny grape flowers cranking out a subtle and remarkable scent.
I walk around for an hour, sniffing flowers the size of
pinheads, trying to find the right word for what they smell
like—lilac? hyacinth? blackberry? trillium? daphne? my
daughter's mysterious teenage-girl-drawer in the bathroom?—
before finally I actually snort a grape-flower right up the old
schnozzertunnel, which causes a sneezing fit, which scares the
willies out of a scrub jay in the next row, who rockets out of
the vines like a blue jet, which scares the willies out of yours
truly, so I close up shop and sit down on a rickety wooden
pallet and contemplate the universe.

The universe, as seen from the top of the Langes' hill, is
rimmed by the Chehalem Ridge, a long hill filling most of the
scene; the rest of it is a humpbacked smaller hill across the
way, most of which is oak and fir but some of which is a
vineyard belonging to the acronymic corporation that owns
half the planets in the solar system. I stare at the vineyard
across the way for a while, thinking how the soil and weather
and latitude and microclime there are pretty much exactly the
same as it is on Jesse's hill, the only difference being about half
a mile and the thousands of little mylar ribbons fluttering
from their wires to keep the marauding birds away.

I have an interesting experiment in mind, I say to Jesse
later, when I have shuffled back up to the winery. Your wines
against their wines, and see if there's a difference.

Yeh, he says, there's a difference.

Why? Same soil type, weather, clones, probably the same hawks floating over the vineyards. The only difference I see is that you use the BirdGard machine to keep the enemy at bay and they use all those nutty ribbons.

Well, yes, that's all true, says Jesse. Different wine-makers, though.

Makes that much difference?

It does, he says, if you have different concepts of what you want in the wine. And while all winemakers making pinot noir from the Red Hills will say that they are chasing after wines that reflect this place, that bring forth the quality and flavor of the grapes, really they all have slightly different takes on what that exactly means. Which is why all the wines don't taste the same. Plus of course the winemakers make

wine in different ways, with different targets in mind. There
are about ten thousand ways to make wine. So the fact is
really that no wine here tastes exactly like anyone else's wine.
There are wines that have a whole array of similar
characteristics, yes, but each one's different. Which is cool,
when you think about it.

Still, though, tasting yours against theirs would be a neat
experiment, right? Because you and Don don't have all that
different an ethic than they do, do you?

As I believe you know, he says, I like everybody.

What, they make a heavier wine? You can tell me.

I'm not going there, he says. But *you* taste one against the
other and tell me what you think.

Emboldened by the mission entrusted in me, I do exactly
that over the next few nights, with the help of my subtle bride,
and I scribble notes and everything, which makes her smile
her enigmatic smile, and I discover that while there *is* a
discernible difference between the wines—the acronymic
corporation's are a little denser and burlier, and Jesse's are a
little more silky and vibrant—the fascinating thing is that
they have the same spicy earthy feel and smell, a gently
peppery and sunny and muscular flavor that somehow seems
to me to be the very salt of the neighboring hills from whence
they came.

I want to dismiss this idea as fanciful wine-geek stuff, but
over the next few weeks we drink a number of pinot noirs
from the Red Hills, and while they come in a variety of
weights, as it were, and indeed as Jesse noted they are all
slightly different, a startling number of them have the same
peppery spicy earthy feeling—a sort of burly confidence, a
dark berry flavor, a lean strength, a kind of . . . I don't know
how to say it. A signature smell, and a flavor so identifiable
that the wine all but speaks up itself after the first sip: *I'm Red
Hills, man. The real deal, the big leagues. Bring it on, Frenchy.*

MORBIFUGE

I GET TO READING MY erudite San Franciscan friend's
musings on French pinot noir, which he enjoys, as he says,
for its range of flavor and character from *darkly spiritual to
sensuous*, which makes me smile, as does his recollection of the
words incised into a stone gateway in Savigny-les-Beaune in
Burgundy, describing the wines of the area: *nourrisant,
theologique, et morbifuge*—roughly translatable as nutritious and
nourishing, provocative of prayer and spiritual musing, and
good for fending off death.

The thought occurs to me, not for the first time, that
reading my friend's work also is nutritious, reverie-inducing,
and life-affirming, for whatever his nominal subject (usually
wine), the true matter under consideration is the Human
Being, endlessly odd, fascinating, confusing, layered, complex,
a cipher to itself, and a roaring mystery and delight.

Also every time I read my friend's work he makes me
hungry, for he has a sharp eye for the pleasures of the kitchen
and a ferocious memory for the meals that went with the
wines he tastes. For example a dinner in 1967 in a wine cellar
in Beaune: partridge tart with a local white wine, salmon with
pinot noir, duck with more pinot noir, cheeses with *more* pinot
noir, cake with champagne, and finally coffee and plum
brandy "into the small hours," as he says politely. Or a dinner
in a vineyard in Burgundy featuring ham, pâté, fish from the
river below, and local boar, accompanied by many wines. Or a
dinner one night near the Red Hills of Dundee which
featured almond and garlic soup, pork and mushrooms, lamb
and cornbread, polenta fritters and cinnamon ice cream, and
many pinot noirs. Or the meal that accompanied what he says
was the most memorable wine he ever had, in more than fifty

years of savoring wines, a nameless wine that haunts him still. He was high in the Swiss Alps one day, on his way to Milan, when he stopped at an inn for lunch. Wildflowers were scattered everywhere, he says, and drifts of snow lay dazzling in the midday sun. The crisp air, the brilliant light, the grandeur of the mountains . . .

At the inn he ate a simple meal, veal and noodles and green beans. "My glass was filled with a light red wine poured from a pitcher, left on the table," he remembers. "I was relaxed, carefree, and happy. Oh, how ruby bright that wine was; it gleamed in the sunlight. I remember clearly its enticing aroma—youthful, but with a refinement that surprised me. The wine was sweetly exotic: lively on my tongue, perfectly balanced, and with a long, glossy finish.

"The young woman who had poured it for me was amused when I asked what it was. It was, she said, *vino rosso*.

"Whatever it was," concludes my friend, "the wine had been made with uncommon care. It was exquisitely graceful. I shall always remember that wine, though I have never learned what it might have been. But the pleasure in wine is subjective: we each bring something to what is there in the glass."

HUMMING

JUNE. ON MY WAY to a town three towns past Dundee I stop by the vineyard and wander for a moment through the old pinot noir block, trying to sketch the new leaves in my notebook, trying to guess which canes Jesse will want to train where next year, keeping a weather eye out for hawks, and wondering if the easy breeze sifting through the vines is indeed between five and ten miles an hour like it is supposed to be.

I am supposed to give a talk in the town three towns away, but whenever I am supposed to give a talk I end up just telling stories, because I have no particular wisdom or expertise or lesson to convey, and am loathe to lecture and suspicious of sermon, and I am only a storyman anyway, absorbed by and agape at stories all the time, so I just tell stories, which is what we all are anyways, walking collections of stories, and as I amble through the fluttering rows I get to thinking of all the stories I have been told amid these vines, wet stories and green stories and funny stories and tired stories and dreamy stories and dusty stories, plant stories and animal stories and people stories, and for a minute I wonder if all those stories soaked not only into me but into the vines and dirt here, so that the dirt is a little deeper and redder than it used to be, having been watered with words, and this thought makes me smile because it reminds me of my sister who is a Buddhist nun who says, We tread only on the rim of things and hardly ever see how much more vast and infinite is the Gift, and her wise words remind me of my boy Billy Blake the great mad poet who says, If the doors of perception were cleansed we would see everything as it is, Infinite, and as I am

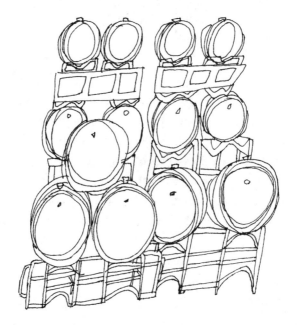

chewing on this remark I come to the end of the row and
notice a big hawk looming over the young chardonnay block,
which makes me happy for murky reasons.

On my way back uphill to my car I remember what Jesse
told me once, that each vine produces enough grapes to make
about three-fourths of a bottle of wine, and I chew on the idea
that three-fourths of a bottle of excellent wine is probably just
the right amount necessary for two or three people to start
telling stories fast and furious, so that each of the vines I pass
is pregnant with stories, some of which were never born into
the world before, and this idea makes me happy also, so by the
time I get to the town where I am supposed to give a talk I am
cheerful as a chipmunk, and start right in telling funny
stories, and after a few minutes I notice an older woman with
tired eyes laughing fit to bust, and I think to myself, you
know, today I didn't totally screw up like I usually do, today I
brought some light to tired eyes, and I drive home humming.

RILLS OF HILLS

JUNE. OUT OF A sincere genuine heartfelt serious yearning for knowledge, a personal itch to add a smidgen of knowledge to a world mooing for wisdom, I conduct a comparative study of pinot noirs from around the world. Over the course of four weeks, and mighty cheerful weeks they are too, my subtle research assistant and I taste holy grails from Germany, New Zealand, Australia, France, Italy, Chile, California, and Oregon. The cheapest of these (from Chile) was six dollars and the most expensive I don't want to tell you or even remember the price because we have children and I should have put that money in their college funds instead of guzzling it but I didn't, being a mule and shoe and a dolt and shoebox of a man.

All in all we tasted some thirty bottles of pinot noir from around the world and while I have no illusions whatsoever about being able to comment authoritatively on the wines, or their respective qualities, or characteristics of the wines by region or nation, or motifs of the wines by latitude, or anything of that sort, I can say, after careful perusal of my scribbled notes, that the Chilean pinots seemed bright and lively and fruity and forgettable, and the Antipodeans were interestingly stony and spicy and peppery but sort of thin, and the Germans were superbly balanced and substantive and superb and horrifyingly expensive, and the Italians were lovely but light, and the Californians were all over the map from fat and fruity to lean and lithe, and so, with all due respect to the German Spatburgunders, which were absolutely terrific but realistically I could afford only two a year unless I sold a son off into indentured servitude, and to one Australian pinot

from the Yarra Valley which maybe made more of an
impression on me because it set me going on a whole
afternoon of ozreverie and australyearning, and with all due
respect to pinots from the Otago Valley of New Zealand
which Jesse had a very high opinion of but I found generally
sort of acerbic and astringent, and with all due respect
especially to the Carneros and Russian River districts of
California, from which we drank some astounding wines and
where I'd really like to visit now and wander through
vineyards pretending to do research, the whole issue of the
Best Pinot Noir in the World seemed to, at least at my table,
at least for one (happy) month, come down to, as Jesse had
many times suggested, Oregon and France.

Which fascinates me. In the vast scheme of things, two
rills of hills riding the same line of latitude, two regions with
the right rain, two districts with distinctive dirt, two small
places on the vast face of the spinning rock where men and
women grow a particular peculiar fidgety grape, and worry it
into fermenters, and sluice it into barrels and casks made from
the ribs of oak trees, and then wait and wait and sip and sip
and consider and ponder and ruminate and wait and muse and
tinker and blend and bottle and savor and slurp and sing; and
some of those men and women, maybe many of those men and
women, deep in their wine-dark hearts, think, without
fanfare, that perhaps, it may be, just this once, semi-
miraculously, that the wine on the table, standing dignified
amid bread and cheese and pears and berries, is among the
best of its kind in the world. Which is a pretty cool.

WINETASMAGORIA

JUNE. I SAY TO Jesse one day, how will you know if you
made the best pinot noir in the world? and he says, with his
usual cheerful honesty, we won't. We *will* know if we made the
very best wine we could have made *that* year from *those* grapes,
but there's no way really and truly to know if it's the best. I
mean, we could enter contests and all, and a lot of people do
that with their wines, because contests and medals and
comparative tastings are great for marketing, and we do that
sometimes, I am not a marketing fool, we have won highest
honors at the Oregon State Fair and been lauded by *The Wine
Spectator* and by *The Wine Enthusiast*, which said bluntly we
were quote one of the great pinot noir producers in the United
States unquote, but in the end this sort of thing is mostly a
matter of opinion, of what you think a well-made pinot should
taste like, which really means what *you* like in a pinot. Which
everybody has a different opinion. As you know from your
weird predilection for heavy pinots, which it totally wrong, as
I have explained.

Or you could, I say, taste every pinot noir made in France
and Oregon that year.

Well, you could try, he says. But I don't think it could be
done. I bet there are ten thousand pinot noirs made every year
in Oregon and France.

I calculate how many pinots you would have to taste
every day to taste a whole year's run, and come up with the
figure of thirty a day for a year, give or take a few, including
two weeks' vacation.

So you could actually do it, I say.

Yeh, says Jesse, and never drink a drop the rest of your life because you would be so sick and tired of pinot. And at the end of the year you would still be issuing your *opin*ion as to which was the best. My point is that, all due respect to wine advocates and wine spectators and wine enthusiasts, it's the winemaker who knows how good the wine is—how well he or she did with what he or she had to work with. So much of it is style and philosophy and experience and intuition. Which is why it's fun, and also why it drives you crazy, and also why so much of the wine industry is sales and advertising and marketing and illusion and phantasm.

Whoa.

Cool word, eh?

Phantasmagoria, I say, word-addled as always.

Winetasmagoria.

Sounds like an island near New Zealand, says Jesse, grinning, and I drive home daydreaming about the Island of Winetasmagoria, its orderly vineyards running down to the bright surf on all sides, the brilliant whitewashed walls of its wineries, its legendary stony spicy sinewy chewy sinuous pinot noirs, the dense dark local bread and sweet figs like small honeyed green fists, the leathery smiling quiet people, the chalky salty cheeses, the green-and-white wooden ferry easing into the tiny harbor, the birds of startling colors, the tapestry of trees, the mounds of fresh silver-blue fish and bright orange-red fruits at the market, the faint music of guitars and mysterious pipes, the glints of sails at sea . . .

THEY WERE JUST KIDS

JUNE. I GET TO talking about wine to a friend who was a
bomber pilot in the Pacific in the Second World War and
he says huh, I'll tell you a wine story. You know, a lot of guys
didn't make it back from the war. A lot of guys sank into the
wine-dark sea. I keep their names in my heart. Guys never
seen again on this earth. Brave guys. Boys, mostly, of course. I
see their faces sometimes, those guys, and I stop whatever I'm
doing and say a prayer. You never know what prayers do. You
just never know. And they don't have any graves really, you
know, those guys, so sometimes now once in a while when I
am having a glass of wine I pour them a glass, you know? To
remember them by. I pour myself a glass and pour them a glass
and sit with them a minute and then pour their wine into the
dirt so that at least one place on earth remembers them that
minute, you know? My garden has drunk some fine wine in
memory of those guys. They were just kids, most of them,
some of them not even old enough to have ever *had* a glass of
wine, you know? But I remember those guys. Good guys. Gone.

We talk about his experiences as a pilot in the war for a
while and he tells me, Some guys when they came back to the
ship from their bombing runs they were so keyed up and
rattled that they had to have a shot of whiskey before they
could even talk, you know? Not me though. I never liked
whiskey much. I like wine. Little bit of wine with your food is
a gift from God and that's a fact. You couldn't have had wine
in that situation anyway. Wine's for thinking and talking, you
know? Like beer. Beer is for talking and laughing. Whiskey's
for when you need a shock to the system, or for finishing off a
great night. You drink whiskey too early, you got a problem,

one way or the other, either you like it too much or you know the cops too well, you know what I mean?

My friend tells me about the night his plane ran out of gas as he and his crew returned from a bombing run on a Japanese troop ship and the plane went down in the cold black ocean and the three men dove into the ocean and scrambled into their life-raft and prayed all night and near dawn were rescued by an American ship which traded them back to their mother ship in exchange for ice cream.

Did you have a glass of wine when you got back to the ship finally? I ask.

Nope, he says. Took a shower, got bandaged up, and went to sleep. When we woke up we got another plane and went back to work. Wars don't wait. Lot of guys didn't come back from that night though. I'll have a glass in memory of those guys tonight.

I will too, I say.

Good man, he says.

A few months later I get a letter in the mail from his daughter telling me that her dad died peacefully and that his wife and children and grandchildren were around him when he died so he died happy. That night I get a good bottle of wine and have a glass in his memory and pour a glass in the garden for all the guys who fought and still do.

WALLS OF WINES

JUNE. DON AND I spend the morning in his basement, which used to be the winery, as he points out, showing me the places in the windowsills where tubes and hoses wore ruts in the wood as he and Wendy pumped the new wine out of the press into barrels outside the window.

A looong time ago now, he says with a smile, as swallows zoom by commuting to and from the birdhouses he's hung everywhere.

I had expected chaos and hubbub in the basement, expected stacks and towers of cases and flotillas of bottles, a cheerful madhouse museum, but the place is meticulous, a photograph of quarterback Don Lange of Marshalltown High, a small wooden table in the middle of the room, four chairs around it, a lovely old guitar on a stand in the corner, and more than four thousand bottles racked from floor to ceiling in redolent pine shelving along three walls.

Man, I thought this was going to be chaos and maelstrom and cheerful disaster, I say.

Well, says Don, it was chaos until recently, when we finally got things under control. Sort of.

Is this every wine you ever made?

O no, says Don, no no. I don't have room for the whites or even for the Willamette Valley pinot noir any more. Now I just keep a selection of the single vineyard pinot noirs and our estate pinot noirs. I hold back three cases of each every year. I let the others go. I do that with regret, because in an ideal world you would keep a healthy selection of all the wines you make, to be able to taste and compare them through the years, they change in such interesting ways over time, you know, but

I just don't have the room. I do have some whites from the past here and there but not too many.

He crouches down in the southwest corner, near the gleaming guitar, to look through the earliest wines, which are dusty and have what you might politely call a busy label.

Man, that is one ugly label, I say.

We didn't know any better in the beginning, says Don, grinning. We hired a graphic artist who was the nicest person you'd ever want to meet but enamored of lots of graphic motifs at the same time, which makes for a crowded label. In 1990 we went to the very simple labels we use now, which have one central image—a rose, a guitar neck, a trout fly—on the clean white background. My feeling is that our labels since 1990 have helped us a great deal, because you can tell it's a Lange wine from across the room, you know the look of our bottle, you could pick out our wine from a whole wall of bottles. Which is a good thing customerwise.

You have any of the first vintage, the 1987s? I ask.

Well, I thought we did, but I don't see any, which isn't such a tragedy, as the pinot gris really *should* be gone, a good gris will last ten years but not much after that, and the chardonnay was made to drink within a year or two, and while the pinot noir from that first crush was very good, as I recall, we have made much better since.

What was the very first wine you made?

Pinot gris, 1987, fermented not in the tank but in barrel, which no one had done at that time.

How was it?

It was *ex*cellent. We got off to a very good start with the gris.

What did you sell it for? I ask, remembering David Lett selling his first bottle for $2.65.

We asked twelve dollars for it, which was sort of outrageous, says Don, but we were trying to make a statement.

We were trying to say *Let's take this wine seriously.* Heck, the Alsatians were selling their wine for twelve dollars or more at the time and I didn't see where their wines were better than ours. So we priced accordingly.

Sell it all?

We did, actually, which was a relief, as you can imagine, because Wendy and I had about twenty cents between us at the time.

We get back to talking about the basement, and how organizing and arranging four thousand bottles of wine was rather like a war, says Don, I'd have to move cases aside to make room for the rack, and then rack some of the wine, and then move some more cases, and it took forever and a day, partly because there was a truly shocking amount of wine down here and partly because each vintage makes you remember the growing year and the process of making it, you know.

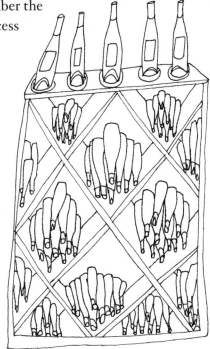

I explain my theory that one of the prime attractions of wine is that it provokes memory and stimulates story and serves as emotional marker, so that a particular bottle or vintage often means more to the consumer than can be easily explained by the elixir itself, and Don agrees vigorously, and this line of talk sets him going on particular years and what he remembers. For example the 92, he says, pulling out a bottle and holding it up to the light to examine the color. That was a really hot year and a really early harvest, which made for a really big wine, a bold wine . . . a little too bold, Jesse would say. And here's an 88, which was a warm summer also but a more moderate year weatherwise, compared to 92 when it was roaring hot and dry all through August and September. Or 87, he says, pulling out a bottle and blowing the dust off, which was another very hot very dry year and a very early harvest. That year was too hot and too dry altogether.

How's the wine?

Well, pretty good, actually, but we had to be very careful in the winery to get a good wine from that harvest, and I felt we had to work too hard, you know? The problem, or the challenge, is to work with what the land and weather give you that year. Ideally you want perfect weather all through the season so you have the best grapes possible to work with.

Or get out of the way of, as your progeny says.

Yeh, but he's being modest, as you know, says Don, smiling. Even with the best grapes and the best soil and the best weather you still have to practice the craft.

And you get better at it year by year?

Well, as with any craft, he says, the more practice you get, the more situations you face, the more experience you get, the more you are able to measure one situation against another in your mind, but then again no year is ever the same as any other, and I can't sit here and say that every winemaker gets better with age, that's just not the case. But in general, yes, the more harvests you go through the more knowledge you have about how to approach and handle a crop. Not to mention the next eighteen months of work in the barrel room. And one interesting thing I have learned is that as the years pass the wines are less susceptible to vagaries of weather because the roots are deeper and the vines are better able to deal with stress. In the earliest years of a vineyard when the plants are babies, as Jesse says, bad weather can cause some of them to just shut down.

Let's keep pulling wines randomly and you tell me about them, I say.

Okay, says Don, here's a 90, that was a great year, a moderate growing season beginning to end. Here's a 93, a year we liked a lot, those were just gorgeous wines. Here's a 94, a hot year that gave us a big wine, like 98, here's a 98, see . . . well, you can't compare the colors in this light really, what we should actually be doing is opening about a dozen of these wines and tasting them carefully, you know. That's what we should do if we really wanted to examine and explore the subtle differences in the wine.

My heart leaps for a moment at the idea of opening a dozen bottles of the best pinot noir in the world *with the guy who made them! who is itching to explain how they were made and why and what creative challenges he faced!* but it's ten in the morning, and I have stuff to do all the rest of the day, and he has stuff to do all the rest of the day, and I say mournfully *aw, I can't,* and he says sadly *me neither,* and we stare at the proud herd of lovely bottles on the table between us for a minute.

We really should do that sometime, though, he says.

Okay, I say, happily.

Well, anyways, he says, pulling a bottle blind from the rack, here's a 97, that was a dicey fall, cooler than we wanted ideally, although the wine turned out to be excellent.

Are there any wines in this room that are *not* excellent, Don?

He considers the walls of wines for a moment and then says, If we had the latitude this morning, with two glasses and a corkscrew and some time, I'd open the 95, that's the only one

I'd feel ill at ease pulling the cork on. Beyond that I feel confident.

Why that one?

Terrible weather at harvest, he says. Horrible weather. A lot of rain and it was way too cold. We worked awfully hard that year to get a good wine but it was still too diluted. It'd be interesting to see how it's changed over the years. Actually I think I will open a bottle of that tonight just to see for myself.

Keep going, I say.

Okay, he says, here's a 99, a very solid year. Touch and go at the start of the growing season, a late start, a very wet spring, like 91, and in April and May we were wondering if we were going to get enough good weather in September and October to make it, but then it was *beautiful* right through Thanksgiving. In fact, looking back on it now, if I had known we would have that kind of weather right through November I would have let some grapes hang a little longer just to experiment. Maybe waited until November to harvest a block or two.

You'd have harvested at Thanksgiving? I ask, reflecting that I have never heard the words *November* and *harvest* in the same sentence before.

Some winemakers, says Don, will let their grapes hang until the very last second, letting them build up to like 30 brix, and then add water when they make the wine, which produces fruit-bomb wine that apparently a certain percentage of wine critics and reviewers and the wine-buying public like.

You don't?

No. That's not what pinot noir should be.

You ever make fruit bombs?

We have made some heavy wines, he says, wines with real stuffing in them, but not by design; we made them in 98, 02, and 03, for example, because that's what the grapes gave us

those years, that's what we had to work with, that's what the
weather produced. Ideally you want a pinot that's got . . .

Structure, texture, balance, I say, and he laughs and says
yes, that's exactly right, and that's exactly why I like working
with pinot noir so much, because if you have a very good
vineyard and a good vintage to work with you can work
endless subtle variations of a really lovely sensuous tactile
varietal—a wine capable of such range that if, say, we were
poaching salmon with a very light sauce we would open the 96
estate, but if we were grilling venison or steak we would open
a 98 estate. Now, both of those wines come from the same
vines and were made by the same two men, but they are very
different wines, which I think is interesting.

If we were going to have a glass of the best pinot noir in
this room, I ask, which bottle would you open?

He turns slowly in the four holy directions, considering
the walls of wines, and then pulls out a bottle and blows the
dust off and holds it up to the light.

94 estate, he says, smiling. There's a wine that has
mellowed beautifully. That would be delectable on its own.

He puts the bottle down on the table with the other
bottles he has chosen from eighteen years of his work on this
hill, and we look at the eager bottles for a long moment, and
then we sigh and stand and shake hands, and walk back out
through the basement, past the photograph of him as
Marshalltown's quarterback, and out the basement door under
the darting swallows, and past the old pinot noir block, and at
the winery door we part company, and head off to do the
things we are supposed to do, but all the rest of that day I
think of that herd of bottles sitting on the table in his
basement, waiting for us.

CISTERCIA

THE RED HILLS OF Dundee, for winemaking purposes, are a sub-appellation of the Willamette Valley Viticultural Area, which itself is most of the northern half of the valley. Appellation-wise, the Red Hills are bounded roughly by the towns of Lafayette (to the south) and Dundee (east), and by Chehalem Creek to the north.

The western boundary, however, is mostly Abbey Road, which is named for Our Lady of Guadalupe Trappist Abbey, which sits calmly on 1,300 acres of wooded hill and sprawling fields just inside the boundary. There are thirty-two men living there, ranging in age from twenty-six to ninety. One of the men there is Father Mark, who has lived alone in the woods for thirty-five years. One of the monks is Father Casey, who is the grinningest man I ever saw and who drops to his knees suddenly when anyone says the word *God*. One of the men there is Brother Eugene, who has made one hundred fruitcakes a day for twenty-five years. One of the men there is Father Martinus, who was born in Australia on the shore of the Indian Ocean but who has lived in the Red Hills now for fifty years and knows more about the Yamhelas people than anyone else alive. One of the men there is Father Peter, who is the abbot, and a most cheerful and erudite man, and one day I drive up to the abbey and wander around with Father Peter.

Well, he says, our abbey here began really in New Mexico, in 1948, when a group of monks from the Trappist community in Rhode Island made a foundation, as we say, in the desert. When an abbey or monastery gets to a certain size often what happens is that a group gathers and goes off to start another community.

Like an iceberg calving? I ask.

Um . . . sort of, he says, smiling. Well, after seven years in the desert the men were satisfied that farming New Mexican soil at altitude was not going to work out so they sold the property to the Benedictines and came up to Oregon where the farming was better. That was 1955. We kept the name of the desert community, Our Lady of Guadalupe, which commemorates the Madonna's appearance at Tepeyac in Mexico in 1531. You remember Juan Diego and the flowers.

Being a Catholic boy, I do remember the story of the visions of Juan Diego at Tepeyac, partly because of Juan's real name, his Aztec name, which was a pretty cool name, Cuauhtlatoatzin, which means the eagle who talks, and partly because of something the Mother of the Lord of the Starfields said to Cuauhtlatoatzin when he was worried about the health of his family: *Put this in your heart, my son: do not be afraid. Am I not here, Me, your mother? Are you not under my shadow, under my care? Am I not the fountain of joy? Are you not in the crease of my cloak, in the fold of my arms? Do you need anything else?*

Which words have always made me feel better as they pretty much cover all the bases, seems to me.

You're still farmers, mostly? I ask the abbot.

Nope, he says. The farm didn't do well. We have a flourishing vegetable garden for our own table, but mostly our income now, such as it is, comes from the book-bindery, which does eight hundred books a week, mostly for colleges and law schools and medical schools and such, and the wine warehouse, and the bakery, which does serious mail-order business. And we have the forest, of course, which grows 600,000 board feet of timber a year and which we harvest judiciously. We have a forester and everything. Young guy. Nicest guy you ever met. We have more than nine hundred acres of woods, you know, which is a sizable crop of timber. Mostly fir.

Back up to those words *wine warehouse*, Peter.

We're coming to it, he says, see, here's the old carpentry shop, where we used to build church furniture, mostly pews, and I note with pride that there was a time we were the biggest church furniture concern on the west coast, we built furniture for the cathedral in San Francisco and for churches all over Oregon and Washington and Idaho and Montana, but then came the reforms of the Second Vatican Council, you know, which were wonderful reforms altogether except that they made church furniture a much more freeform thing, no more accepted conformity of design with pews, for example, so pretty soon we were losing our shirts. We tried making office furniture for a while there but it didn't take. Well, our Father Pascal had a brilliant idea, and he proposed that we use a corner of the old shop to store some of the wine being made by the fledgling new wineries in the Red Hills. I think there were eight wineries here at the time, and their problem was that once they made and bottled their wine, they didn't have room to store it safely on their premises between the time that they bottled it and when it needed to be shipped. So we entered gently into the warehousing business. And then came the explosion.

As Abbot Peter finishes his sentence he opens the nondescript door of the nondescript former carpentry shop and my jaw about falls on the floor, because all around me from floor to faraway ceiling as far as my eyes can goggledly see there are thousands and thousands and thousands of cases of wine from the Red Hills. There is, no joke, an ocean of excellent wine here, in the biggest enclosed space I have ever seen, an interior that doesn't appear to have an end; the vast stacks and towers of wine recede undiminished into the distance like a dream.

Peter? How many bottles of wine are here?

Oh, two million easy, he says. Capacity is 300,000 cases, but the first rule of storage and easy access is that you never want to be at full capacity, for fear you wouldn't be able to accommodate a client, so I'd guess we are at 200,000 cases or so, which is 2.5 million bottles, eh?

My mind sputters for a moment and we walk on, Peter narrating.

There are more than ninety wineries represented here, including our neighbor on the other side of the ridge, Susan Sokol Blosser, whose white wines are over . . . there, he says, pointing to a wall of wine the size of an aircraft carrier. Most of what we have here is red, I would guess, and most of the red is pinot noir, for reasons you understand, given the soil and growing conditions in the Hills.

I am still agog at the towers and turrets of wine and I stammer for a moment before asking Peter about warehousing competition.

One small competitor, he says cheerfully, an old pie factory in McMinnville, but we're not too worried.

One very good thing about the warehouse operation, he goes on, is that all the management and staff are neighbors, which is good for everyone, because there really aren't that many jobs locally, you know, and we like to provide a little direct assistance for our neighbors as well as praying for them.

Have you thought of growing grapes on your land and making wine? I ask. I mean, you *are* in the Red Hills appellation, and what an income source that might be, eh? Trappist Abbey Pinot Noir Reserve sounds pretty good.

We've thought about it, sure, he says, but beyond the question of labor and investment there's the fact of the land. We face the wrong way. Our entire property is on the west side of this long ridge above us, and beyond questions of incline and such the fact is that it just isn't the best spot for growing grapes of any kind. *Never* isn't a word I'd use for the possibility but *unlikely* is a good word.

We walk all the way through the warehouse, Abbot Peter greeting everyone, and we walk past the place where he began his own life as a Trappist monk, lacquering pews at age twenty-five, and we talk about his tenure as abbot, eleven years so far, on an indefinite term, which when I ask what that means he grins and says, Until I am seventy-five or deceased, although as a community we review the idea of me as abbot every three years, and so far the idea of me as abbot hasn't been rejected out of hand.

We talk about monks and wine, and he notes that the Trappist community at New Clairvaux in California, on land once owned by Leland Stanford, is now growing grapes and bottling tempranillo, zinfandel, graciano, syrah, and trebbiano, and of course, he notes, we were founded originally in Burgundy, which makes a fairly decent pinot noir.

Do you and your fellow monks drink wine at all?

We do on solemn feast days, he says, you know, Christmas, Epiphany, the Annunciation, the Immaculate Conception, John the Baptist's birthday, my birthday . . .

What do you drink when you drink wine? Pinots from your neighbors?

Not usually, he says. Usually wine from boxes and bags. We're not much for drinking wine, actually. Saint Benedict, whose rule of living we follow, was pretty straightforward about wine: *Monks should not drink wine at all,* he wrote, *but since the monks of our day cannot be convinced of this, let us at least agree to drink moderately, and not to the point of excess, for wine makes even wise men go astray.*

That's mighty perceptive.

Benedict was a very insightful man.

It's sort of incredible, I say, that you have two million bottles of some of the best wine in the world here, and you don't touch a drop of it.

Well, says Peter, we do have generous friends. Recently for example a winemaker friend of ours sent us seventeen cases of his wine for our consumption as we saw fit.

What is it?

Abbot's Table, from David O'Reilly. A blend of nine wines: cabernet sauvignon, merlot, cabernet franc, zinfandel, pinot noir, grenache, syrah, malbec, and counoise. A wonderful wine, rich and lively. David's from Ireland and he makes a little of it every year in memory of the claret on the family table when he was a boy.

What will you use it for?

Making new friends for the abbey, he says. We are in the middle of a ten-million-dollar capital campaign to restore and renovate and update the place and care for the older men, and the Abbot's Table may help with conversational flow.

By now we have walked through much of the abbey and its doings, and I have taken more than too much of Peter's time, whereas he is a man devoted to a life of prayer and contemplation and his time is a great gift, and we pause by the front gate to shake hands and bow, but as I prepare to step back into the world I find myself with another gift: a bottle of Abbot's Table 2001. The last I see of Peter as the gate closes is his smile, hovering in the bright air like a prayer.

TRIPLE SEVEN

July. I WANDER UP to the vineyard and Jesse and I walk through the old pinot noir block, talking about the heat. It's a hundred degrees today, and it was 103 the other day, and my friend Arron at Domain Drouhin told me it was 106.4 over there, says Jesse. It's shocking. We're two weeks ahead of where we are usually. Color change, at this rate, will be in four to ten days. So we might harvest in early September, which would be the earliest ever. We've already hedged twice and might do it one more time—hedging being the trimming of the vines to let air and light into the rows; vines in intense light and heat like this grow wildly, and would, if allowed their heads, create a green thicket so dense the berries would starve for light. So we give them haircuts, he says cheerfully, showing me clippers like scissors for giants.

We wander through the old vines talking about how this is really the best year ever at Lange because all the vines on the whole hill are mature this year and producing fruit, even the baby chardonnay vines at the bottom of the hill, and last year's weather was so perfect for pinot noir that the wines in barrel in the winery should be superb, and Jesse says he's confident that they have all the right clones growing in the right places, and he explains about clones, and how pinot noir produces thousands of clones, because it's such an unstable swooning movie star of a vine, but some of those clones are sort of the gold standards for pinot, and those are generally the ones planted if possible, like here where rows 1 through 16 of the old block are Wadenswil, which makes a wine with a sort of a chocolate feeling, he says, and Pommard, which makes a wine with a sort of vanilla tone, those are rows 33 through 48 at the bottom, and the rows between are Bien Nacido, which was developed in California and so is a clone especially suited to climate conditions on the west coast. What's your favorite clone? I ask.

Well, I like everybody, he says grinning, but the Pommards have a round lush ripe spicy wild meaty feel that's fun to work with, and the Wadenswil has an upright angular flinty rocky minerally character that's fun to work with, and both characters are true representations of grapes from this soil. Those clones come from the Cote d'Or, ultimately. People call them Dijon clones, and we use, specifically, clones 113, 114, 115, 667, and 777, and of those I like 115 and 777 the best. I guess if I had to pick a single clone that I like the best I'd pick 777.

But you like everybody, I say, teasing.

Yeh, well, the thing is, says Jesse, for me, as a winemaker, I have a lot of things going on in the back of my head at the same time. Making wine from one clone isn't that hard. I mean, duh, yeh, it's hard, but it's straightforward, you know? and ultimately not as interesting as working with wines from several clones. So our estate wine has some of that big feeling of the Pommard, and some of the stony muscle of the Wadenswil, and the wine we make from a combination of characters, all of which reflect this place this year, is to me way more interesting than one wine from one clone. And that's the theory with all the grapes we buy. Wally's old block of pinot noir is Pommard, the Freedom Hill grapes we get from Dan are Wadenswil, and the grapes we get from Ken Cancilla, the west wall grapes as you call them, those are from *all* the clones I named. We know who grew what and we keep mighty close track of what's what and where at harvest. You'll see.

PUPINOT

JULY. WHEREAS WE GOT a puppy a while ago and the puppy is one wild adventure I spend a lot of time with the puppy, and one roaring hot afternoon I come home from work and find no one home but the pup, my subtle research assistant being off somewhere doing something and the children off somewhere committing mischief and misdemeanor, and whereas it's been a really long day and it's stunning hot, the pup and I sprawl and loll in the grass with a bowl of water for her and a glass of clean crisp pinot blanc from Lange for me, the new wine just released a month ago, a lovely clear penetrating wine that carries cool peace right down my throat into my old moaning bones.

This is damn fine wine, I say to the pup, who yawns.

Don't yawn at me, dog, I say. This is excellent wine, and I'll tell you why, and you will be edified and educated, which is what you need, seems to me, because all of life is not bounding around chasing food and biting people and dreaming about sex. Some of life is contemplating and conversing and cogitating and admiring creativity in the human animal, which is a fascinating animal, not so much because of its capacity for language or philosophy or abstract thought, as some say, but because of its endless possibility for grace and generosity and epiphany. Seems to me that animals of my species are more capable of creativity than animals of your species, which is maybe why I am sitting here with wine and you are sitting there with water.

The pup knows the word *water* and her ears and eyebrows do that startling-awake thing they do when she hears words like *food* and *walk* and *treat* and *ball* and *bad girl!* and *no!* and *get down from there!* and *my god don't eat that!* and *why don't you do me a huge favor and pee outside like the boys do?* which I have said to her many times even though my sons tell me it's too much of a rhetorical question for the pup to handle easily.

I get her another bowl of water and get myself a second sip of the wine and make a mental note to tell Jesse that the new pinot blanc is an excellent wine to have while talking about moral evolution with your dog.

SUMMERSTUNNED

J ULY. I WANDER UP to the vineyard and there's no one there
at all—no Chuy among the rows, no Gabriel in the tasting
room, no Kelly in the laboratory, no Don in his office, no Jesse
in the barrel room, no Laura in the winery, no Wendy
marching by with her brace of dogs like hairy curious
quadrapedallic bodyguards, and so I wander back out into the
vineyard and amble among the rows. For a moment I wonder
where exactly everyone went, and I have a vision of a
chardonnay tank exploding and vast delicious gasses
steamrolling the staff and tumbling downhill to the highway
where traffic squeals to a halt [*chardonnay emergency in Dundee,
film at eleven!*], but then the flittering speckled spackled
playful hot nutritious healing light gets to me, and the
murmuring and muttering of the leaves, and the way in which
a man hidden amid many rows of tall grapevines on a steep
hill is about as hidden as you can possibly get in this world,
and I discover that I am awfully tired, for any number of good
reasons, and I lay myself down in the warm red dirt, grasses
tickling my ears, my head propped up against a sturdy old
pinot vine trunk as thick as a baseball bat, and I contemplate
and pray, and consider and ponder, and ruminate and cogitate,
and muse and meditate, and utterly lose track of time, and
enter a summerstunnedness I have not felt since I was a small
boy musing in tall grass bathed by salt air reading the same
book five times over and considering the birds of the air who
did not sow neither did they reap.

I lay there between rows 11 and 12 in the old block for
what seemed a very long time, dazed by the light, not thinking
at all. The vines grew, the insects conducted their intricate

geometric maneuvers, birds
of various hues and screecheries zoomed by,
a hawk quartered the hill overhead, summer simmered. After
an hour or two I heard polite bootsteps nearby and Chuy
poked his head around the corner of the row and saw me and
he smiled and didn't say anything and I smiled and didn't say
anything either and he vanished and I stood up creaking and
dusty and happy and put my life back on like a jacket and
ambled back up to the winery which now miraculously
hummed and buzzed and bustled with people sowing and
reaping. I didn't say anything to anyone about the chardonnay
emergency (*film at eleven!*) and no one asked me why I was
covered with fine red dirt.

THE THIRTY-MILLION-DOLLAR HILL

J ULY. ON GENERAL PRINCIPLE, feeling that I should as a
professional journalist diversify my sources and triangulate
my tale, I wander up not to the Lange vineyard but to other
vineyards in the Red Hills, and spend the day ambling and
shambling and basking and sipping and listening to a
remarkably erudite and cheerful and courteous raft of young
people tell me stories about wine and the making of wine and
the peculiar adventure of making wine in these peculiar hills.
I visit Sokol Blosser Winery, run by the cheerful Susan Sokol
Blosser and a crew of fresh-faced quick-witted fellow
adherents to the idea that terrific wines can be made totally
organically, and I visit Archery Summit, where the gracious
young tasting room manager Sari White walks me through
her winery's single-vineyard pinot noirs, all from grapes grown
half a mile from Lange vineyard, you could throw a rock and
hit Jesse from here, she says, grinning, and I visit Cuneo
Cellars, where owner and winemaker Gino Cuneo has built a
bocce court and dreams of making an Oregon nebbiolo, and
then I visit Domain Drouhin Oregon, which occupies, as
Susan Sokol Blosser noted with a wry smile, the Thirty-
Million-Dollar Hill.

At Domain Drouhin, Jesse's friend Arron Bell walks me
through the tiered winery, built by the legendary Drouhin
family of France to fold gracefully into the steep hill so that
trucks and tractors bearing grapes at harvest enter the top
floor and then juice flows down into tanks and barrels on the
floors below, *the first winery built as a winery in the whole state*, says
Arron briskly, and *as tall as an eight-story building*, he says, and
there's an eighty-foot drop from roof to bottom floor, he says, and he

walks me through the tank room, which features tanks the size
of office buildings, stern gleaming enormous creatures with
vast gleaming bellies filled with superb wine, and he walks me
through the barrel room, filled with endless alluring rows of
barrels filled with superb wine, *eighteen thousand cases of wine a
year,* he says, and we sip through five of the wines made on the
premises, and we discuss the weight and texture and structure
of pinot noir, in which complicated and subjective matter he
turns out to be firmly and insanely on Jesse's team, maintaining
that a great pinot noir should be both substantive but also
lively and bright, perfectly balanced between the poles of
pinotpossibility, and I educate him as to the desirability of
pinot that leans decidedly toward muscle, and he politely refuses
to be educated, young people these days being so adamant
about their ignorance, and we discuss pinots from these hills
that he and Jesse find too strong and heavy, which I carefully
record in my notebook for later surreptitious purchase, and we
discuss chardonnay, which he says Oregon is finally getting
right after thirty years of the wrong clones which, he says, gave
the state a reputation for grassy lemony greeny weedy wine
that didn't sell well for the wholly understandable reason that
it wasn't actually any good, and we talk about how the legendary
Drouhin family of France came to be harvesting ninety acres
of chardonnay and pinot noir in the Red Hills every year,
beginning in 1987 when Robert Drouhin bought one hundred
acres of hillside here, and we talk about Robert's daughter
Veronique, who makes all the wines at Domain Drouhin
Oregon even though she lives most of the year in Beaune with
her husband and children, she's here usually two or three times
a year for a week or two at a time, says Arron, she's always here
for harvest, and we ship wine to Beaune by Federal Express
fairly often so she can see where we are with it, and she brings
the children over a good deal, or used to, three of our wines are

named for her children, you know, Cuvee Louise and Cuvee
Laurene and Chardonnay Arthur, and we talk about how the
purchase of Dundee dirt by the legendary Drouhin family of
France accorded instant and enduring worldwide winehead
respect for the Jory soils of the Red Hills, and how after
Beaune bought into the idea that Oregon might actually be a
place to make the Best Pinot Noir in the Whole Wide World
everybody and their third cousin jumped in, says Arron, it was
like the official wineworld stamp of approval that people like
Dave Lett and Dick Erath were right about pinot noir here,
and land prices rose precipitously, and winemakers from

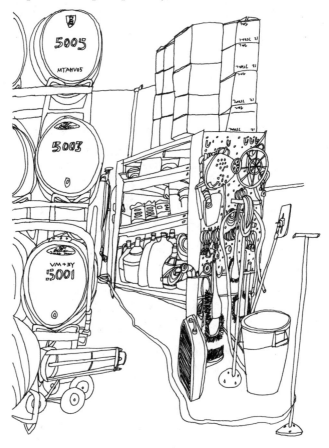

California and Australia and New Zealand and Germany and France and many of the United States bought Oregon land, and now, almost twenty years later, things have changed economically and culturally and landscapingly in the northern Willamette Valley, no question, and it is a very interesting thing indeed to be involved in what really is a sea change in the life of the valley, going from 150 years of one kind of agriculture to a different kind of agriculture, but the second kind, vineyard agriculture, carries a whole different array of effects than do, say, hazelnuts. I mean, he says, people don't drive out for the day to taste their way through new releases of hazelnuts.

Good point, I say.

We get to talking about wine libraries and wine archives, and I mention Don's basement, which appears to be the bulk of the Lange wine library, the museum where some of every wine he and Jesse ever made is stored, and Arron tells me about the meticulous Domain Drouhin wine archives, with sixty-six six-packs of every wine made there since the first bottlings in 1988, and we talk about how Veronique's mother Francoise comes over at harvest also and cooks for the entire harvest crew, and O my *God*, what a cook, says Arron, she makes these amazing lunches that make you moan with satisfaction and then you have to stagger out into the vineyard again, but you need all those calories because you are totally working your tail off at harvest, and we talk about harvest for a while and he agrees utterly with Jesse that you have to sort of get into training for it for a few weeks beforehand and then come down from it afterward like it was an expedition or a voyage or something as he says, and we get to talking about how good beer is a crucial ingredient for making good wine, and how he personally himself is a devotee of Full Sail Rip Curl Ale, from Hood River, Oregon, and Mirror Pond Pale Ale, from Bend, Oregon, having researched many excellent beers carefully, and we further get to talking about the tools and implements and miscellaneous equipage of the vineyard and winery, and I tell him grinning about Jesse and the pusher-downer tool, and he smiles and reports that at Domain Drouhin Oregon, the westernmost outpost of the ancient and legendary and multi-multi-millions Maison Joseph Drouhin wine empire of France, boat oars are used to push down the fermenting pinot noir muck, which pleases me inordinately for some reason.

Are you going to make your own wines someday? I ask. Arron Bell Winery?

O yes, absolutely, he says. You could make a really excellent sauvignon blanc here, I think, and it would be very interesting to work with pinot blanc much more than most people do, and I think syrah might do very well here, and of course our chardonnays should only get better and better. Pinot noir is the calling card, the bedrock, the foundational wine, but there's a lot of room for creative experimentation, sure. You want to get Jesse going sometime, ask him what he thinks he could do with chardonnay. I mean, yes, every winery in these hills is after great pinot noir, and some of them are making amazing pinot noirs, but one of the cool things about making wine is that there's always room for improvement, for different styles, for creativity.

Which wineries are making the most amazing pinot noirs? I ask.

O no no, says Arron, grinning. I'm not going there. No no.

C'mon, I say. Life's short. Be bold.

I'll tell you who makes amazing pinot noirs, he says. Domain Drouhin makes amazing pinot noirs. Want to taste some more?

Jesse always says *I like everybody* whenever I ask him a question like that, I say.

Jesse is a subtle man, says Arron.

A CERTAIN ELEGANCE

JULY. I WANDER UP to the vineyard and get absorbed again by the packaging and containment of the wine, the corks and bottles and labels and barrels and casks and boxes, and I note that the labels all have photographs of roses or guitar necks or trout flies on them, the whites bearing yellow roses, and the workhorse Willamette Valley pinot noir bearing a red rose, and the estate pinot noir, the wine from this red dirt, bearing the neck of Don's guitar, and the rest of the pinot noirs bearing various trout and salmon flies, which were tied by an artist named Judy and presented as a gift to the winery in honor of Don's total addiction to fly-fishing.

Are the particular flies chosen to reflect a particular characteristic of that wine? I ask Don.

Sometimes, he says. Sometimes I just like the fly, but we put the Papillon salmon fly on the Yamhill Vineyards pinot noir to indicate a certain elegance. It's one of the most beautiful flies there is and the wine is lovely. Later I check Jesse's Web notes for the wine with the Papillon fly on its face, the wine made only with grapes from Wally's vineyard: ". . . traditionally the most elegant of the three vineyard designates we produce each year . . . the vineyard is above the town of Yamhill and lies at an elevation of 400 feet . . . the soil is Willakenzie and the grapes are produced by eleven-year-old Pommard clone vines. Bouquet is dried cherries, vanilla, peppermint, strawberries; caramel and coffee flavors on the palate are carried by balanced and structured tannins. A wonderfully complex and pleasing wine that we recommend with fresh salmon, pork, and rabbit . . . only sixty cases released."

Wandering away from the pile of labels stacked by the bottling machine I get absorbed by the bottles themselves, which are from the California Glass Company and the Pacific Coast Container Corporation, which are corporate cousins, and which together sell all sorts and sizes of jars and bottles, all of which are made by the Owens-Illinois Company, which started in 1888 when a kid named Michael Owens went to work blowing glass in Toledo, where fifteen years later he invented an automatic bottle-making machine, which changed the world of wine, not to mention the packaging of a vast array of other things, and today the Owens-Illinois Company is pretty much the biggest glass company in the world, with 38,000 employees on five continents, including Australia and New Zealand, where it also makes the bottles for the local pinot noirs, which fascinates me, the same vast corporation hatched in Ohio bottling the same kind of wine in different *hemispheres*, hmm.

The boxes everywhere evident at Lange are white and sturdy and made by the Georgia Pacific Corporation, which is

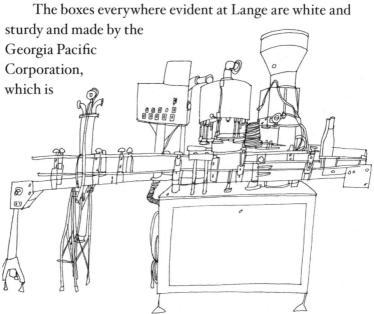

yet another fascinating story, having been invented in 1927 in a ratty tin shed by a kid named Owen Cheatham as the one-man one-room Georgia Hardwood Lumber Company, which then boomed so far and so fast that it eventually became the biggest supplier of wood to the Allies in the Second World War, and the biggest employer in Indonesia, and one of the biggest timber companies in the world, so powerful that it had to split up by order of the federal government, and today the company hatched in a ratty tin shed in Augusta employs 55,000 people worldwide, and hauls in twenty billion dollars a year making and selling all sorts of things, among them toilet paper and toilet-seat covers, but it still grows and mills mountainous quantities of wood, and owns millions of acres of America, including a vast swatch of the Coast Range hills twenty miles west of Lange Winery, from which the wood pulp for Lange's boxes does not come.

I think it comes from Louisiana or Arkansas or something, says Jesse. Which is sort of ironic, I guess, considering that we now ship our wine to Louisiana and Arkansas, so their trees end up carrying our wine to their tables.

Which are probably made from wood from Oregon, I say.

It's a great country, says Jesse.

TRACTOR-HUM & HOSE-THRUM

JULY. I STOP BY the vineyard just for a minute on my hurried harried way to Somewhere Else, and to cool out mentally and eat some fat slabs of sunlight I sit for a while on an old barrel at the back of the winery, and as I lean there half-dozing like a cat and keeping an eye out for hovering hawks Gabriel rushes by and he says grinning *you are getting to be a regular fixture around the place,* and he says this on the run so the end of his sentence trails off as he recedes and I smile at the remark, and at how it diminishes at the end like a train whistling west, but then a minute later I realize with a pang that I *don't* belong here, that this *isn't* my place, that it's my place only glancingly while I am telling this story, and that when I finish telling this story the place and its people will fade away from me like Gabriel's voice, and that this loss is inevitable and inexorable, and that even though I'll stop by here for years to come it won't ever be quite the same, that the vines and dirt and sun and hawks and voices and insects and tractor-hum and gravel-rattle and bottle-clink and barrel-boom and hose-thrum and sun-stun won't mean the same things to me, won't sing the same song, won't speak the same language they speak to me now.

So for a moment I am sad and rueful; but then the sun is adamant about *its* story, and I see a redtail hawk the size of a small airplane, and I think, not for the first time and not for the last, that this is what happens to people and stories, you sense them and collect them and tell them and savor them and then you and the stories move along down the road, sometimes together and sometimes not.

When I finally slide off the barrel to get back to Getting To Where I Am Supposed To Be, there's a wild scramble and scrabble in the grass and leaf-litter a few feet away as a rotund ground squirrel sprints away from what he or she must have thought was some particularly shaggy and bespectacled part of the winery; and I drive away grinning and thinking about how the ground squirrel might tell that story tonight: *I was just poking around for nuts and berries when suddenly this totally monstrous giant One of Them rose up and I hightailed it, man, I booked and boogied and blew out of there right quick, because you never know what They will do, I could tell you tales that'll make your tail twirl . . .*

HISPANOREGON

VERAISON, OR COLOR CHANGE. The grapes, heretofore a bright and cheerful green, are turning pink, red, redder, even light purple here and there.

Takes about two weeks for all of them to change over from green, says Jesse as he hustles by on his way to taste barrels with Don.

What's the crew doing out there today? I ask.

Leafing, he says. Pulling leaves off carefully to make sure each cluster is getting light and air. As the grapes change color we want to be sure they have every chance to mature properly.

Who's the crew?

Those are Ezequiel's guys. I talk to Ezequiel and he recruits his own guys. Today leafing, tomorrow spraying sulfate.

Why?

It's been so wet this year that I want to be sure, especially now, that there's no mildew, no fungus, no mold. They'll go through the whole vineyard and give the vines a light dusting just to make sure. I'm a little nervous. The conditions are just right for mildew and we can't afford it.

He fades away to the winery and a minute later Ezequiel walks by and we talk a bit. He is a sturdy dignified man very aware of being at work. He is of Mexican ancestry, as are all the men in his crew. Some years ago, he says politely, most of the Hispanic labor force in the valley was seasonal, following the grape and hop and hazelnut and berry harvests, but one effect of the wine boom in Oregon over the past twenty years has been to provide year-round work for those who wish to do it, which he does, and he now is manager of a crew in great

demand among winemakers not only in the Red Hills but all
through the valley, which is why he carries a cell phone, and
why, as Jesse told me, one of the most important aspects of the
general manager's job at Lange is scheduling Ezequiel and his
men for planting, vineyard maintenance, and harvest if
necessary.

You enjoy the work? I ask Ezequiel.

I like to work, he says. Work is important.

Are they always the same men in your crew?

No. Sometimes some, sometimes others. Men I trust.

Are they all from Mexico?

They all live in Oregon, he says politely.

I'm interrupting your work, Ezequiel. Thank you for
talking to me.

Thank you, he says. Yes, I must go. Thank you.

Later I read the endlessly interesting stories of numbers.
Today there are some 350,000 people of Hispanic descent in
Oregon, about 10 percent of the population. The Hispanic
population of the state grew by 71 percent from 1980 to 1990,
144 percent from 1990 to 2000, and 20 percent more from
2000 to 2005—the same quarter-century during which the
wine industry arose and blossomed in Oregon. In the past
fifteen years, the labor force of Hispanic men ages eighteen to
forty-five in Oregon has grown by 270 percent, three times as
much as in the rest of North America.

Every county in Oregon has seen more than 100 percent
growth in Hispanic population except three of the most
remote counties—Baker, Harney, and Gilliam. The largest
numbers of Hispanic people live in the most populous
counties (Washington, Multnomah, Marion, Clackamas, and
Lane), which are the counties that make up most of the
northern Willamette Valley. The county with the lowest rate
of Hispanic poverty is Yamhill. Among Hispanic people in

Oregon ages eighteen to forty-five—the prime demographic for physical labor—60 percent were male, with an average age of twenty-three. Ezequiel's crew, I'd guess, had an average age of about twenty-four.

I wander through forests of numbers, thinking about how numbers are actually families and clans and stories and meals and fourth-graders teaching their grandmothers how to use e-mail and new houses in new developments and the first applications to college in the whole history of the family for untold generations and sweatshirts with the logos of rock bands and such. Some of these numbers are Ezequiel and the young men of his crew.

Near the end of my pawing and ruminating over numbers I come across the most interesting number of all: the rise in percentage of college degrees earned by Hispanic women in Oregon has risen by 430 percent in the last forty years. *Viva la Mexicana.*

BLOWING IN THE WIND

A UGUST. I ZIP BY the vineyard for a few minutes on my way to Somewhere Else and catch Don loading his truck with guitars and amplifiers and fishing gear and such and he's sort of in a hurry because he and Wendy are supposed to be heading to a music festival in central Oregon near the town of Sisters, which is named for three nearby mountains, which are named Faith, Hope, and Charity, but I ask him how he got started playing music and his face lights up and he stops loading his truck for a minute and says,

Well, I actually remember the moment that made me want to pick up a guitar. I was driving along in Marshalltown in a 1948 Ford and the Dylan song "Blowing in the Wind" came on the radio, the Peter Paul & Mary version, you know, and that was it for me. Blew my mind. Went and got a guitar and started trying to figure it out. Still trying to figure it out.

You still have that first guitar? I ask.

Nah. I do have the guitar I toured with, though, a 1940 Martin, that's the one down in the basement with all the wine. That's a good guitar. That guitar has made a lot of music, some of it good music too.

Now that he's relaxed for a minute I ask him a question I have always wanted to ask but never found quite the right conversational opening for: Why in heaven's name do they have goats rambling out behind the house?

Hmm, he says. That's Wendy's domain. They just came by about a year ago and they just stayed. They wandered up here one night from God knows where and they never left. It was kind of weird to suddenly see goats looming around the house in the darkness. We thought they were deer or coyotes.

We tried to catch them in the beginning but they are a lot quicker than they look. Wendy fed them so they stayed around, but they are mindless chewing machines, you know, and I worried about the vineyard, so we fenced them in behind the house there, where they ate the apple tree.

They ate a tree?

Sort of. They debarked it to the point where I'm not sure it'll recover.

Do you like the goats?

I like the goats from a distance, he says, grinning. Wendy, however, really likes animals and they like her. She's an animal person. Me, I like our dogs. The goats, well, not to be rude or anything but there are a lot of excellent recipes for roast goat that would go very well with an estate pinot noir. That's what I think.

What would Wendy think of that?

Wendy would say we better be on the road sooner than later, he says, smiling, and he hustles off to finish cramming his truck and I drive away thinking about a thick garlicky goat stew with olives and good bread for dipping and grapes and pears and cheeses and two glasses of pinot noir and then half a cigar while watching for the last swifts and the first stars.

MARTINUS

ONE DAY WHILE WANDERING on the grounds of the
Trappist Abbey in the Red Hills I meet a man I have
long wanted to meet: the legendary Oregon historian Father
Martinus Cawley, who is a Trappist monk and who grew up in
Perth on the western shore of Australia and who has been for
years perhaps the most astute and learned and eager collector
of stories of the Yamhelas people who once graced these hills.

Martinus is cheerful as a bird and wears a floppy hat to
keep the sun off his shining pate and he starts right into
telling stories and later he sends me some of the stories he has
written of the People.

The ridge behind the Abbey was, he notes, the dividing
line between the Tualatin clans to the north and the Yamhelas
people of these hills. There are many spellings of Yamhelas,
among them Yam Hill, Yamhill, and Chehalem. These hills
were reported to have fairly sparse timber in the survey map
of 1852, as the Yamhelas conducted seasonal fires to enhance
the berry crops. They also harvested acorns in oak forests and
gathered wapato tubers from the lake that used to be nine
miles north, Wapato Lake, which isn't there anymore, it's
been drained, but it's still a floodplain for the Tualatin River,
which tries to fill it up once in a while.

The gathering of vegetable foods fell mainly to the
Yamhelas women, says Martinus. In one hand she would carry
a small conical basket, into which she would drop each acorn,
berry, or tuber that the other hand plucked. When the basket
was full, she would toss its contents into a woven bag worn on
her back and held in place by a strap passing around her
forehead. The Yamhelas had no pottery but were so skilled

with the various fibers available to them that they could make waterproof baskets and conical helmets to keep off the winter rain. The baskets, by the way, were used not only for soaking raw foods but also for boiling them. They did not, of course, set the combustible basket over a fire, but they filled it with water and carefully lowered into it some well-chosen and carefully heated stones. These would bring the water to the boil for long enough to cook the food. Boiled wapato tubers did not keep well, so they ground them with a pestle and mortar and roasted or baked them into cakes for winter use. Roasting was done in a pit-fire. The pestle and mortar were made from local basalt. They were also used for grinding small seeds.

To harvest the potato-like wapato tubers at the lake, says Martinus, the woman would wade in and skillfully break them off from the stems with her toes and let them float to the surface. She would then toss them into the basket on her back. In contrast, the underground bulbs of the camas plant had to be dug for with a slightly barbed stick. Berries, of course, were eaten raw or dried in the sun and preserved for later use. The Yamhelas also ate the deer that abounded here, and fished, especially for salmon. They also made annual expeditions to the ocean to dig for shellfish.

As for weapons and tools, says Martinus, let me just mention the small hunting bow, made of yew wood, and as for playthings, let me mention the elaborately carved smoking pipes, and also the gambling dice of various kinds—interesting traditions in the light of the casinos that nowadays help to finance the Confederated Tribes of the Grand Ronde.

The Yamhelas were given to spiritual retreats, he says, in which the retreatant would retire to a clearing on a sacred place, usually a hilltop, and there await signs and wonders. Often the sign would be the arrival of an animal, which the retreatant would study carefully. The actions and antics of the animal, which was taken to be a totem or messenger, would inspire in the retreatant a new song and a new dance, which would thenceforth embody the rhythm of his or her new approach to life, and the animal species involved would serve as a personal totem, to be treated with special veneration. One such hilltop is the land on which we stand, and I like to think that this hill has lent itself to such sacred and spiritual and songlike purpose for time immemorial. We Trappists ourselves, upon arrival in Oregon in 1955, did not hesitate to make the most prominent spot on its crest our own holy place in celebration of Our Lady of Guadalupe.

The first white people to settle on this hill, says Martinus, were Thomas Jefferson Hubbard and his wife, Marie Samato. Marie may have been Iroquois or she may have been Chinook—no one is quite sure, although it does not appear that she was of the Yamhelas people. We do know that Thomas and Marie were married in 1837 by the pioneer Methodist missionary Jason Lee. Marie died in 1909, when her age was guessed to be ninety. Thomas died in 1877, at perhaps seventy-four years old. We do not know much of

Thomas except his facile mastery of his blacksmithing trade, his eagerness to face any challenge, and a remarkable ease in making and keeping good friends. Though he claimed no religious preference, we know he gave generous hospitality to passing clergy, including a freelance preacher of a religion of love, who was apparently shunned by all other clergy as too easygoing.

This makes me laugh, because Martinus is a professional and I am an amateur in a religion based wholly and solely on the idea that love is the first and greatest rule, and his clan has been devoted to the idea for nearly a thousand years since its founding in the pinot noir and chardonnay vineyards of Dijon, and while I wince to think how often the religion we both admire has been cruel and stupid and craven and greedy and criminal, I am proud also of the innumerable times it has housed tremendous grace and courage and humor and people sprinting with all their might toward holy generous joy; people like Martinus, with his floppy hat and broad grin. The last time I saw him he was riding his bicycle through the echoing cavern of the abbey's wine warehouse, laughing.

THE RIGHT PERSON IN THE RIGHT JOB

AUGUST. I WANDER UP to the vineyard and amble around and after a while I realize there's no Wally. This is odd. Wally is ubiquitous, Wally is a basic thread in the fabric of the place, tinkering with machines, leading impromptu tours of the vineyard, talking laughing commenting pontificating muttering, puttering around with casks and corks and tanks and labels and the bottling machine and the fermenter and the tractor, but today the place is noticeably Wallyless, which is weird, so I ask Jesse where's Waldo? and for the first time since I have known Jesse he winces.

Wally's not with us anymore, he says.

What?

Wally's not with the company anymore.

He quit?

No.

I digest this for a moment and Jesse looks uncomfortable. Did you . . .

No. It was an amicable parting, believe me. Wally's been with us since the beginning. He and my dad go way back. Wally's not here now. He's a great guy, and he did great work for us, and we'll always buy his grapes, and I really like the guy, but he kind of made his own schedule, and we can't do that any more. It's time to tighten up the organization. The company's growing and maturing. It's not a mom and pop operation anymore. It's a family business that grew out of our basement—we were in the basement for *twelve years* before we built the winery—but my job is to fine-tune the company, to make sure the gaps are filled in, to manage the corporation. So there have been some changes recently. Laura left to be a yoga

teacher. Kelly left to work with another winery. I hired an
assistant winemaker, a young guy from California, Nathan.
The tasting room is in good hands now, and the vineyard, and
the winery, and my dad can concentrate on making the wine,
and I can concentrate on managing the business. I've been
here six years now and I've learned a lot. I've matured a lot.
The business and I have sort of grown up together. Now I see
where I fit. A first-generation business wants to stay status
quo, you know? But you can't stay status quo. Status quo
changes all the time, especially in the wine business.

There's a Bruce Cockburn song where he sings *the trouble
with normal is that it always gets worse*, I say.

Yeh, says Jesse, that's right. And a company that wants to
stay status quo starts to sprawl. It gets larger than it should in
places. Gaps develop. So my job really was to fill in the gaps. I
wanted to raise the profile of the company nationally, and get
the tasting room running smoothly, and develop a wine club,
and develop a steady market for futures, and get our events
schedule running smoothly, and make sure the vineyard and
winery ran smoothly, and build national distribution of our
wines. We should be sold in every state. Maybe not a *lot* in
every state, I'm realistic, but we should be available
everywhere. That's just sensible for the business, market
variety. And why not us? You're at a restaurant in Omaha and
you're curious about this Oregon pinot noir that everyone's
talking about, why not us there on your wine list? Or in South
Carolina and Vermont and Texas or wherever. And that's
happened. We sell in twenty states now. I'm proud of that. We
just got North Dakota this morning. I spent a lot of time on
the road interviewing distributors, and getting us on
restaurant wine lists, because people who taste our wines in
restaurants will want to buy bottles at their local store, and
they should be able to. That's what a national sales manager

will worry about, and that's the one position I have to hire someone for still.

So then what? I ask. For you, I mean.

Well, says Jesse, I haven't really been away from the winery for five years, other than business trips, and I don't think two days a week off is out of the question. I'd like to get back to New Zealand and work a harvest. I just bought a house in Dundee and I'd like to putter around with it and work in the garden and have barbecues and such. I'd like to spend more time fishing. I mean, you know, I'm twenty-six years old, and I've spent five solid years learning how to manage people, and managing people is

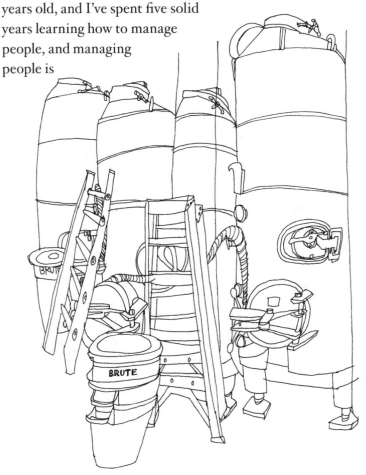

really difficult. Making wine pales by comparison. So one thing I tried to do is get people doing the work they should do. The right person in the right job. Wendy's great at financial stuff, so she takes care of banks and loans and licensing and lines of credit and mortgages and real estate and such, and Nathan will take care of data and equipment and he'll learn vineyard management, and Gabe runs the tasting room, and Chuy takes care of the winery, and the crew takes care of the vineyard, and I manage the company and make wine, and my dad is freed up to do what he does best, what he does better than any of us, which is make wine.

He's great at it? I ask.

He's unbe*liev*ably great at it, says Jesse. He's got the gift. Remember one time you asked me if I was going to be like every other young winemaker in the valley and make small expensive cult bottlings of my own wine? Answer: no. I want to make great wine with my dad. He's really good at it, and there's so much to learn from him, and it's cool to work with your father on something you both really like and are good at. Not many guys get that chance.

Good point, I say.

Plus maybe we'll make the best pinot noir in the world, says Jesse, grinning.

The holy grail, I say.

Yeh, the mad crusade.

Maybe you already made it, I say, only half teasing, thinking yearningly of their pinot noir from three hillsides, my favorite Lange wine of all, a dark deep thoughtful sinuous wine.

Nah, says Jesse. Not yet. You can always do better. That's what's cool about making wine. Next year's weather will be different. No two years are ever quite the same, so the wines are always a little different. There's so many things go into making wine—the soil, the weather, the harvest, the winemaker. There's always room for improvement. Which is pretty cool but also drives you nuts. Which is why I am taking off this weekend to the Deschutes River to catch the wily steelhead.

I notice a cooler the size of a refrigerator in his truck. What's in there, the polar ice cap? I ask.

Mostly sausages and cheeses and beer, he says. There's a good deal of beer. I'm meeting two friends who are in medical school and they need good beer. Good beer is *very* important. You can't have enough good beer on hand. Winemaker's adage: it takes a lot of good beer to make good wine.

Any wines in the cooler?

Yup, he says. An Argyle sparkling wine, the 1999, which was a very well-made wine, and some 2000 Bordeaux Saint-Emilion, because this trip is a special annual occasion with these guys, and that's a wine to savor. And a couple of our reserve chardonnays. I'll put our chardonnays in the river. Nothing like a Lange reserve chardonnay chilled overnight in the Deschutes River. Draws the wily steelhead to the wily fisherman. Little-known fact. I should note that on the label.

What wine will you drink with the wily steelhead if you catch the wily steelhead? I ask.

Ah, says Jesse, if I catch the wily steelhead, then we will open these, and he opens the cooler to reveal two bottles of Lange 2002 estate reserve pinot noir.

A very well-made wine, I say.

Hmm, he says. Winemakers who maybe didn't screw up terrific grapes.

RECKLESS ABANDON

AUGUST. I WANDER UP to the winery and for once do not speak to a human bean but instead spend hours reading the labels on the bottles and the notes on the winery Web site, all of which are written by Jesse, so in an odd way I spend an afternoon at the winery listening to Jesse without Jesse being actually technically present, Jesse being actually corporally in New Hampshire that day, as he tells me later, the highlight of which business trip was an adamant woman in Portsmouth insisting, after a few glasses of Lange wines, that Jesse endure a blind taste test of his wines by vintage to see if he could taste the different years, which he could, to her amazement but not to his, because, as he said to her politely and says to me a little less politely, I mean, you know, I helped *make* the wine, so it's not like it's really that amazing that I would remember it, wines really do have slightly different characteristics every year, and you would think that the person who helped grow and blend and bottle the wines would *know* the wines for heavenssake, but she was astounded, I think because she thought I was too young to know what I was doing. But: she was wrong.

This makes me grin, for I had long ago come to the same conclusion, partly from perusing his Collected Works, the notes he writes for labels and Web posts, in both of which genres he strikes an informative but friendly tone, essentially the same pitch he sounds in person—factual but relaxed, professional but eager, workmanlike but salted still with the energy and enthusiasm of the young. Sometimes he seemed an old soul to me, a youth graven with gravitas, his duties and responsibilities weighing worrisome; but then his usual curtain of businesslike reserve would slip for a moment, and he would say something hilarious, or I would see something— the shocking chaos of his truck, for example, inside which it seemed a drunken heavy metal band had lived for several years—and realize once again that the general manager of the corporation was a guy in his twenties, a very astute businessman indeed but not so old that he would be averse to bagging work for a few days and going fishing with a cooler of excellent beer.

For example a high-summer Web post: "Summertime has arrived with reckless abandon here in Oregon Pinot Country. Temperatures are right around 85 degrees, blue skies abound, and the vineyards are mid-bloom. This important stage of self-fertilization is the last move the vines make before the berries become berries and the clusters begin forming into true fruit. All in all, this growing season is shaping up to be a week or so ahead of schedule. . . . We've already thinned some clusters, with more to do closer to veraison (color change), and we've dropped all of the 'shoulders' from our clusters as well. We'll check crop levels after bloom and set are complete and adjust our thinking accordingly to keep our yields around two tons per acre. We just wish the growth of the vines would slow down a bit during the salmonfly hatch on the Deschutes River in central Oregon."

TOENAILEHREEERRAHDOOO

A UGUST. I SPEND A cool dark humming morning in the
barrel room, where the fans hum quietly keeping the
room at a steady 60 degrees even though outside it is a searing
glaring 90 degrees, and I wander among the mammoth oak
casks, and trail my fingers over their ribs as stout as horses,
and examine their hoops made of chestnut withes and
galvanized steel, and ponder the holes called bungs, and read
their provenance, their cooperages, the redolent woody
woodshavingish workshops where they were born: Allary and
Vicard, Saint Andre and de Bourgnogne, Francois Frere and
Tonnellerie Radoux, and I get absorbed by the words
Tonnellerie Radoux, and chant the sounds quietly for a
minute because they seem so utterly and tonguetwistingly and
alluringly French, toenailehreeerrahdooo, and Jesse wanders
by and asks me if I have finally lost my mind altogether, which
he figured was certainly going to happen but not until harvest.

Tonnellerie Radoux, sounds like a French actress, doesn't
it? I say. Not yet famous but starting to be noticed, and soon
she will star alongside Gerard Depardieu in an incomprehensible remake of an old Hollywood B movie, which will give her
career a terrific boost, and then she'll have a much-publicized
fifty-hour marriage, and be arrested in Toronto for carrying
dope in her shoe, and make an incomprehensible art film, and
end up marrying a software baron and eventually running a
cult winery in the Cote d'Or and living in a villa on the Island
of Mustique.

Uh, yeh, if you say so, says Jesse.

We get to talking about barrels and casks and oak staves
and chestnut withes and the many sizes and shapes and

carrying capacities of barrels, and how all the oak in all the
barrels in all the wineries of the world is white oak, and how
coopers make not only oak barrels but also oak tanks and
chips, because some wineries put oak chips in their wine for
flavor but not us, says Jesse, and bigger wineries use vast oak
tanks to store their wines but not us, he says, and we talk
about how generally barrels are made from oak trees in France
or Lithuania or Estonia or Latvia or Ontario or Belarus or
Poland or Minnesota or Missouri or Virginia or Pennsylvania
or lately Oregon, and how Canadian oak adds hints of anise
and fennel flavors to wines, and how American oak adds hints
of vanilla and coconut, and the best barrels are still the French
ones, which is why we have all French barrels, he says, because
there's something about their oak that's just right especially
for pinot noir, and then we get to talking about how long
barrels last, which isn't that long really, he says, maybe three
years tops, and they can get moldy so easily, which is why we
mostly use new barrels, which are expensive, up to eight

hundred bucks a barrel, and why we clean 'em meticulously all the time, which is another one of those winemaking things no one sees, how many hours you are just *cleaning* stuff, and we talk about the withes on the barrel, which are called head-hoops or quarter-hoops or bilge-hoops depending on what they are hooping, and the lid of the barrel, which is called the head, and the lining around the head, which is called the chime, and the lining around the chime, which is called the croze, and we talk about barrel sizes, how there are generally two sizes, the Bordeaux, which is fifty-nine gallons, and the Burgundy, which is sixty gallons, although says Jesse whiskey people use a fifty-gallon barrel for their whiskies, and we talk about how the Burgundy barrel though one gallon bigger is actually shorter end to end than the Bordeaux barrel because it was originally designed for the slightly smaller doorways of wine cellars in Burgundy, and we talk about why barrels are shaped like they are, which is, says Jesse, partly so we can roll 'em and spin 'em fairly easily but more so because when they are racked and stable any sediment or impurity in the wine drifts down to the bulge or bilge or belly of the barrel, which is good because all that muck, which is called the lees, stays in one place and we can take the clear wine off the lees, which is what you want to do.

Uh, yeh, if you say so, I say.

DREAMLINES & SONGLINES

S EPTEMBER. A LMOST HARVEST. T HE grapes are the
darkest blueblackpurple I ever saw, a color that's hard to
find a word for, and the days are brilliant hot and the nights
crisp and cold and Don and Jesse wander through the vineyard
plucking grapes and chewing them ruminatively and carrying
clusters up to the lab to measure sugar and acid levels and
conferring quietly with each other in shady corners and
muttering words like *brix* and *tonnage* and I stay out of their
way, sitting quietly on a barrel and watching and listening to
the winery on the cusp of the World Series and Super Bowl and
World Cup and Grand Final of winemaking.

It seems to me, as a student of how people prepare for Big
Moments, that we are complicated mammals far beyond easy
ken, far more entwined and entangled and engaged with ritual
and prayer and superstition than we understand, so that very
often we face Big Moments with a flurry of propitiatory and
placatory gestures, we lay out clothes and tools, we murmur
ancient chants, we pace dreamlines and songlines, we wear
lucky socks and carry lucky pebbles, we touch the outstretched
hand of the child in the third row for luck, and we walk out
onto the brilliant field, into the chapel, onto the gleaming stage,
nervous and thrilled, ready for the magic moment to be born.

I ask Jesse about ritual and preparation and magic
incantations and songlines hovering invisible over the red dust
of the hillside and he looks at me oddly and says, Yeh, well, we
prepare, that's for sure, for three or four weeks before harvest
you eat more and sleep more, and I work out harder, because I
know from experience that I am going to be going all day and I
want to be physically ready for it, and I guess as far as preparations
in the winery, yeh, we get everything clean and ready to receive

the crop, and there's a lot of scheduling and planning and arranging who is going to be where when, although there's also a lot of scheduling for deliveries of grapes from elsewhere that happens at the last second, this is why God invented cell phones, you want to have the grapes trucked here as fast as possible after they're harvested, but you also want them to arrive staggered, you know, and you want to have the deliveries timed, insofar as possible, to fit our harvest schedule. Every vineyard manager has his or her own take on what's the exact right moment to bring in the fruit, so part of my job is to coordinate their idea of the right moment with our idea of the right moment, and there are a lot of right moments. You follow?

Yeh, I think so. Must be a madhouse here during harvest.

Yup. But it's thrilling too, says Jesse. I mean, you've waited all year for these days, and when they are looming into view it's like you can hear a low drumbeat coming, and when they come it's wild and exhausting and exciting. And it's different intense every day, and different intense every year, so it's never the same. Which is pretty cool.

What are you up to today?

Getting fermenters down from the barn up the hill and cleaning and inspecting them. Getting tanks and bins ready. We just bought a twelve-ton press and we have to get familiar with the settings and get it and everything else in the winery cleaned and in tip-top shape. Harvest is no time for something to break down although something always breaks down at harvest, you can bank on it. We're basically clearing the decks today and for the next couple weeks. We're mad busy but it's a good time, you know—it's what you wait for all year, it's the culmination of the whole year in the vineyard, and also by the way everything and everybody and the whole business and our careers depend on it.

No pressure there, eh?

Just a little. But it's a ball, really. You'll see.

ON THE ROAD

SEPTEMBER. I WANDER UP to the winery to sit on a barrel
and try to smell Harvest Intensity in the air and as I am
sitting on the barrel taking notes Jesse wanders by and we get
to talking about my writing, and I tell him that while I am a
journalist by vocation, I am an essayist by avocation, because
the essay is the coolest form there is, and it's the form in
which I tell stories most easily and naturally, and I explain
that a writer is lucky if he or she finds the form in which his or
her voice flows naturally, and for me that streambed is the
essay, which is why my books so far have been collections of
essays, although I just wrote a book about the muddle and
miracle of hearts that isn't *tech*nically a collection of essays,
although to be honest that book is actually built as a pile of
little tiny essays, and now I am off and running talking about
something I like to talk about, which is Me, and I explain that
after I finish whatever it is I am writing about the vineyard,
which I am not sure what it is exactly because I have learned
in my old age to just follow the thread of interest and worry
about the shape later, anyway after whatever it is that I am
doing here in the vineyard, which is mostly as far as I can tell
spending many hours listening to some nut in his twenties,
after *that* I am going to finish my novel, because every writer
has a novel on the blocks, either in his or her mind or half-
made in his or her typewriter or computer or whatever, the
world is filled with half-novels, in fact someone young and
footloose and energetic could make millions from publishing
the millions of half-novels in the world.

Uh, yeh, right, says Jesse. You ever write a travel book?

Not yet, I say, although I've been thinking about it since
Australia, and then he gets called away by yet another tense

pre-harvest Pressing Matter, and I sit there for a minute
musing about travel narratives as a form, and the great ones I
have read, like the beautifully engraved wanderings of the
forgotten Irish genius Robert Gibbings, or the gentle salty
South Sea island wanderings of the Americans James Hall and
Charles Nordhoff, or the thoughtful wet wanderings of the
Scot Robert Louis Stevenson through the mountains of
France with his French donkey, and I consider how the very
best of travel narratives are not really very much about
physical travel at all but about emotional and spiritual travel,
and the riveting miraculous painful hilarious sweet savage
complicated holy stories of children and women and men you
meet along the road, and suddenly I realize that in writing
about this vineyard on this hill and these people I *am* actually
writing a travel narrative of a sort; a journey through time, a
long voyage around and under and over fifteen acres of red
soil, an expedition through seas of stories here, in this one
place in the wide world.

And too, I think, hunched silently on the barrel, this is in
a real sense a personal journey for the narrator, who used to be
so confident and cocky about the world, and so sure of his
place and role, but who now in his middle years has retreated
from any confident management of his hours and wishes only
to be attentive, to attend to the ocean of grace under duress,
to collect and share stories as prayer and salve and gift, to
accomplish nothing so much as mercy and tenderness.

I am myself a journey, halting and fitful and so often
becalmed.

At home, later, quiet men speak to me of traveling well: *a
journey is best measured in friends rather than miles*, says the
peripatetic American Tim Cahill, and *all journeys have secret
destinations of which the traveler is unaware*, says the Austrian
mystic Martin Buber, *and the whole object of travel is to see your*

own country fresh, says the London storyteller Gilbert Keith
Chesterton, and *the use of travelling is to salt imagination with
reality and to see things as they are*, says the Staffordshire
storyteller Samuel Johnson, and *the longest journey is the journey
inward*, says the Norse mystic Dag Hammarskjold, and *it is
better to travel well than to arrive*, said the Nepalese man who
was born able to speak and stand, and who walked a short
distance in each of the four holy directions moments after his
birth, as flowers arose where his feet had trod, and who told
his mother that he had come to the world to free children and
women and men from suffering, and who was named
Siddhartha by his mama, which means He Who Has Attained
His Goal, which was, it seems to me, to accomplish nothing so
much as mercy and tenderness. And all these years later—
twenty-five centuries after flowers sprang up where he walked,
twenty centuries after a gaunt Palestinian Jew swore that life
defeats death and love defeats murder and hope defeats
despair, fifteen centuries after a Meccan youth flew to heaven
on a horse and returned with the law that kindness is all,
seventy centuries after the voice of I Am Who Am stunned
nomads in a desert—suffering is still the country in which
everyone lives; yet we still all travel toward tenderness,
knowing, deep in our hearts, that it is the only destination
that matters.

A TREMENDOUS MANDATE

S EPTEMBER. As I am whirring and whistling by Dundee I pop into the winery for a second to check some facts and figures with Jesse and I catch him in a rare philosophical and metaphysical mood for pre-harvest and as we sit in the sun by the old block he gets to talking about not only his role with the corporation but moral responsibility and such, and we have about as direct and haunting a conversation as we have ever had.

The thing is, he says, that I am as proud of the fact that we have a well-run operation as I am of the fact that we make very good wine. There are a lot of operations that aren't run very well. There are some wineries that are just ego gigs. There are some that run at a terrific loss every year and the owners don't care. There are some that are just badly managed. There are some where the people who work there don't like working there. There are a lot that will go out of business. But there are some, more than a few, that make excellent wine and they're good companies, you know? I like that about us. I feel like I did a good job so far, and I learned it on the fly too, all due respect to my business education, but it couldn't prepare me for the reality of running a corporation like this.

And you a mere twenty-six years old, I say.

Twenty-seven now, man. Makes all the difference. Now I am ancient like you.

We get to talking about stewardship of the soil, respect for the land, organic practice, minimal use of chemicals on crop, dry farming as opposed to major irrigation which would be sucking yet more water from a public water supply which is oversubscribed as he knows very well not only in his capacity as general manager of a corporation in the county but as the recently elected youngest member of the county water board, and he suddenly waxes eloquent, so much so that I make him repeat what he says, which is: Look, working this hill is a tremendous mandate, a tremendous responsibility. As an American citizen, as an Oregon citizen, I feel motivated to make the most of this opportunity, this incredible gift. To not squander it or let others squander it, you know? I have to be responsible morally, culturally, environmentally. We've been given a gift beyond price—this land, these resources. You can't take that for granted. Well, you *can* take it for granted, people do that, let's face the facts, but not me, and not the people I respect and admire here. My generation in the valley has been given a legacy to uphold, to care for, to improve upon with all the creativity and respect we can muster, and I am damn well going to do that.

That's very well said, I say, and he looks at me to see if I am teasing as usual, but for once I am not teasing, and I say so, and then to my own surprise I find myself saying that to be completely honest about things, Jesse, I am going to miss these conversations, I mean I'll stop by the winery here and there and come

to tastings and releases and such, but the thing that's been the most fun and the most moving is how casual conversations about vines and vats and stuff have turned into conversations about ideas and convictions and dreams, and that's what I'll miss, dammit, because those are the conversations in life that matter, and after this project's done we won't have the same reasons to have these conversations, which is a bummer, because I have really enjoyed them, and soon enough I'll be into some other nutty project and you'll be flying to New Zealand chasing after the Olympic field hockey player.

He grins and I grin and he says quietly, Yeh, I know what you mean. This has been fun. And you know one thing I have discovered? I didn't know how I felt about some things until someone asked and was willing to listen. So thanks.

No worries, mate, I say.

Too many worries, man, he says. Harvest looms.

A CHEERFUL REDOLENT WHIRLWIND

SEPTEMBER. HAAAARVEST! JESSE CALLS me late one afternoon and says cryptically *it's on* and again I beg him piteously to let me come watch, I'll sit on a barrel, I won't move, I won't speak, I'll just be eyes and ears and Roman nose, and he says nope, no way, not during the opening days, I hafta go now, but I will call you the minute we are over the hump and at that point you should zip out here because it'll be safe for aliens like yourself but still intense and you will get the drift of the thing, and I say okay, and he hangs up, and I try to keep in mind that he is actually intensely at work making the product that puts food on his table and I am only pursuing stories for my own amusement and edification, and I consider not for the first time that essentially our relationship is that I am selfish and he is generous, and in a real sense I am thieving time from him whenever I ask him a question, because answering the question takes time away from him actually running the business, and this line of thought occupies me the rest of the day, during which I spend a lot of time thinking about how a lot of what I do as a professional journalist is to steal from people and distract them from doing what they are doing, I mean even if you look at it in the best light, that I am collecting and telling stories as a sort of active prayer for the holy hubbub of human beings, that I am in the business of idea exchange, which is a good and nutritious thing in the universe, and perhaps the seed of real peace and progress and holiness, the fact is that I still am also politely (for the most part) bugging people, and tugging at their shirts like a little boy, and making them pause from the paths they are on, and do mind dumps for me without substantive recompense, I take their stories and make them mine and mill them for my own entertainment and minor cash, and what do they get from the transaction?

Not as much as I do, that's for sure.

This bothers me a good deal and I plop the problem on the table that night in front of my subtle wife.

Hmm, she says. Look at it from Jesse's point of view. First off, he's a courteous young man, obviously not averse to sharing stories and explaining his craft. As you say yourself at tiresome length, people *like* to tell their stories, people are *itching* to tell their stories, and some part of *your* craft and *your* reason for being is to be open to stories, to elicit stories, to savor stories. That's a good thing. People are honored that you listen to them and savor their stories and celebrate their work and share their stories with readers. Secondly Jesse is no dope, and he is well aware that what you write ultimately will be of some direct assistance to the winery, right? I mean, at the very least, more people will know about the wine and the winery than did before, so your collecting and telling of their stories will probably lead to more people trying their wine and visiting the winery. So that's good. So quit moaning and pass the wine.

She's right, as she often is, although sometimes she is *so* egregiously wrong I could tell you bloodcurdling stories, but even though she's right on this particular matter I still chew it and stew it, and later that evening I reflect that if I was *really* a cool guy sensitive to the needs and desires of other people I would go nowhere near the vineyard at all during harvest, and leave the Langes père and fils to their hard and crucial work, and only courteously ask about it afterwards when they have time to draw breath, and besides I have visions of people throwing pusher-downer tools at me, and of being dunked headfirst in a fermenter by people crazed with exhaustion and

adrenaline and excellent beer, but then two days later I get a
call from Jesse who says cheerfully, Hey, come on up
tomorrow morning, we went over the hump last night but we
still have probably four days to go, this would be a good time
to see what happens at harvest, c'mon, we need you to witness,
so I wander up the next morning, on what appears to be the
most crisp clear brilliant sundrenched birdsung hawkhovering
day in the history of the world, and I find the winery a
cheerful redolent whirlwind, fermenters everywhere
fermenting the new pinot noir, towering stacks of just-
delivered chardonnay grapes teetering dangerously, Chuy
steadily working the crusher, Don pawing through the white
grapes intently, Wendy on the phone, Gabe on the phone,
Jesse in the lab checking delivery schedules, pickup trucks
rumbling and grumbling up the road delivering vast stacks of
grapes.

Hey, man, I say to Jesse.

Hey, he says. You ready? Here we go. Watch out for
trucks. Let's start in the old block. Keep your eyes peeled.
There's a lotta stuff going on at once and I don't need you
getting squashed by a truck or something. If that happens we
will just add you to a fermenting tank for a little inky flavor in
the wine.

As we pass down through the familiar rows, now bereft
of their precious clusters, I note that Jesse isn't kidding—there
are about ninety things going on at once, and everywhere I
turn there is activity, all of it purposeful and graceful, as if a
huge sweaty machine smoothly in high gear. Far below, in the
bottom rows, men are picking the last of the estate grapes;
each man wears two white plastic buckets, and they move
along the rows in a quick scuttling crouch, their hands
snapping clusters deftly from the bottom of the vines and
dropping them gently in the buckets. Their stance seems

oddly familiar and I puzzle over it for a moment before it comes to me: men milking cows, their backs bowed to the task, both hands at play, their faces intent, the holy food flowing into a bucket.

At the ends of the rows the men have already picked are stacks of bins readied to be ferried uphill to the winery. Midway up the hill is the tractor ferrying buckets to the winery. At the winery there are buckets and trays everywhere, towers of them outside by the basketball hoop, towers of them inside by the crusher, towers of them still in trucks waiting to be unloaded.

How do you keep track of all this? I ask. How do you know what grapes are where?

Insanely careful scheduling, says Jesse. Also each tray is marked, see, and he shows me the scrawled coded symbols on the trays, indicating kind of grape and originating vineyard: FH CH (Freedom Hill chardonnay), E PG (estate pinot gris), etc.

And how long do you go at this pace?

Different every year, says Jesse, and depends wholly on the weather. Two weeks, three weeks. Cooler wetter weather will compress your harvest, and warm dry days will extend it. In general we expect clear dry Septembers, but you never know. The harvests from 1996 through 1999 were long affairs because Septembers were clear and dry and hot and we could push harvest out a little—there were a couple harvests in there that went for like five weeks. These last couple years though it's been wet and cooler than we would ideally like at harvest so we push to get it all in.

How many tons of grapes are you bringing in?

All told, from our hill and from the other vineyards, about 170 tons. Which is either absolute capacity for the winery or slightly over capacity.

Wow.

Well, that sounds like a lot, he says, but there are far bigger wineries, of course. And those tons are not here all at once. They're moving through. Harvest is more of a process maybe than people see. Which is why it's so insanely busy today.

Take a minute and walk one batch of grapes through in your mind from picking to barrel?

Hmm, says Jesse. Okay, say it's a batch of our pinot noir grapes. They're picked by hand and placed, *not* dropped, gently in the bucket. The picker will sometimes make sure they're ripe by tasting one from the cluster—when they're ripe they're sweet and rich and balanced flavorwise, and when they are not quite ripe they're a little bitter. When his bucket is full he leaves it on the bin at the end of the row for the tractor. Each picker picks maybe a hundred buckets a day. The tractor hauls the bins uphill to the dump tray. The grapes are sorted by hand into the crusher-destemmer machine, and then the whole gluck, called the must, goes in the 1.5 ton fermenting bin, see all the fermenters around, there's like fifty of them here. At this point the ratio of skins to juice is very high, because what you want is extraction—you want the juice to get all the flavor characteristics and structural elements possible from the skins—tannins, flavors, color. In a sense the character of the wine to come begins right there, with the juice getting everything it can from the skins, color and flavor and the backbone of the eventual wine, sort of.

Then you just leave it alone and let it simmer? I ask.

Nope, says Jesse. You do let it rest overnight, making sure the temperature is fairly low, usually about 55 degrees. Then the next day you look at yeast levels to make sure it's ready to ferment properly. There are natural yeasts on the skins to begin with and then we add a little yeast to make sure the batch is ready to ferment. That's called inoculation. And you start pushing the cap down and through the juice with the pusher-downer tool, because you want to be sure the juice is getting every possible bit of extraction from the skins and guck. After that it's pusher-downer three times a day. You get shoulders like a wrestler working in a winery, nobody knows that.

And then into barrel that day? Next day?

Nope, says Jesse. Seven days, on average. You sort of feel it out. We taste it, look at it, gauge the cap, and then finally when we feel it's ready we put what is now the new wine into the oak barrels and rack them and wait. Some will be in barrel a year, some eighteen months, some almost two years. Depends. The reserve wines are generally in barrel maybe sixteen months. That's another whole aspect of making the wine, the constant testing and tasting of stuff in the barrel as it ages, to check color, to see if it's lively and bright, to gauge the acids, to see where the fruit went, as it were. But that's all later, after harvest, and I remind you that we are in the middle of harvest right now, so I have to get moving here, okay? You're on your own, wander around if you want but watch out for trucks and tractors. Probably safest if you just grab a corner somewhere and keep your eyes peeled.

By this point we have looped back up to the winery and Jesse slides away smoothly like a Cheshire cat and I take his sage advice and sit on a barrel at the top of the hill where I can see bustle in every direction, trucks trundling up the road with grapes from other vineyards, pickers milking vines below me, pusher-downers being wielded like heroic oars in the round white curraghs of the fermenting tanks, the little forklift tractor growling far below, the rattling groan of the crusher-stemmer machine . . .

I sit for hours listening and smelling and watching as the vineyard and winery seethe with energy and red dust and faint voices and the snarl of engines and the wheedle of cell-phones. I watch the pickers pause for the briefest of lunches at the ends of the rows, their faces sweating. I watch Jesse sprint by talking on one cell phone and punching buttons on another. I watch truckdrivers inch their trucks backward down the slope behind the winery and unload their mountains of grapes. I spend a few moments counting yellowjacket wasps and give up after a hundred. I watch the goats behind the house and notice that they are not paying the slightest attention to the whirl of activity around them but instead are concentrating their assault on the apple tree. I watch the pickers finally call it a day in midafternoon and trudge up the hill and stretch their backs before piling into their pickup trucks to go home. I watch as Jesse and Don give some sort of quiet signal that draws the bustle of activity into the winery where the crushing and stemming and pressing and sluicing and pusher-downing goes on even as russet dusk crawls up the hill like a brown blanket. I keep an eye out for hawks but over the course of the entire day, all the way from early morning to twilight, when finally I shake hands with a dusty tired Jesse and get back in my car, I do not see a single hawk.

How late are you going to be here? I ask Jesse.

Probably midnight, if everything goes right. Two or three in the morning if something goes wrong.

You going to have a beer at midnight to celebrate a good harvest day?

Not tonight, he says, smiling a little. I'm too tired. At this point what looks really attractive is bed. If I can get four or five hours of sleep tonight I'll be a happy man. That beer will taste fine when it comes, and it'll be there sometime in the next few days. Not tonight though.

Thanks for letting me hang out today.

Pleasure.

Luck tomorrow.

Thanks, man. Pray for sunlight.

Call me when you're all done, okay? Beer on me.

Now *there's* something to look forward to, free beer, says Jesse, and he walks back into the winery, and I drive off into the velvet dark, the winery as lit up and busy behind me as a carnival bright against the black fence of firs.

OR NOT

O VER THE NEXT TWO weeks I talk to Jesse every other
day, just checking in by phone and cell phone and email
to see how harvest is going, and I make notes from our
conversations about the arc of harvest, the narrative of the
thing, and flipping through my notes later I see what he means
about how the opening days of harvest are a sprint, a mad
headlong getting-in and immediate processing of the crop,
and making sure all the equipment is clean and the systems
are in place and everyone knows what they're doing; it's like
the opening days of a baseball season or something, as
teammates get used to each other and develop rhythm and
style and swing and confidence, and then there's a middle
period to harvest, days when everything is zooming along in
high gear, fruit pouring in, fermenters seething and
simmering, crushers and presses chugging all day long, all
machines smoothly in use at the same time, crews and staffs
tired but sure of themselves and easy in the singing chains of
their tasks, and then there's the mysterious
magical hump day, after which suddenly the
end of harvest is actually conceivable, and
then there are the last few days, during
which as Jesse says you have to be *extra*
attentive and *extra* careful because people
are so tired they can get careless, and then
there's the last day, which never actually
seems like a big deal, says Jesse,
because harvest just sort of slogs
to an end finally and everyone
wants to go sleep until spring. It's

like you don't fully grasp that harvest is actually over until a few days *after* harvest, he says, and when you finally grasp the concept you want to have a big party, which is what we do every year with the harvest party.

The last day of harvest this year comes in October, and Jesse is so tired that he can barely rise to his usual dry humor.

Man, I got to bed last night at three and I think I was up at five, he says. I'm done in. But it's a heck of a vintage. These are going to be superb wines, mark my words. I tell you, this harvest and last year's were the two most intense and difficult and complex harvests ever, because of the rain, but we got everything in and everything's in tank or barrel so we're okay.

You lose weight this harvest?

Eight pounds.

That the most ever?

Nope, he says. Lost ten pounds last year. But this year I could stand to lose eight pounds because you remember I was in France for two weeks this spring, doing tastings and all, and going to lunches and dinners with winemakers, and I had to eat so much I thought I would explode. I mean, really, I came back to the States thinking that if I even heard the word *fromage* again I'd scream.

This made me laugh, because Jesse is a lean and sturdy guy who looks more like a wrestler than a cheesehead, but I had to admit that he looked drawn and exhausted.

Man, I better leave you alone and let you hibernate, I say. I'll pop back up in a couple weeks to talk.

I might be awake and alert by then, he says. Or not.

GOOD ON YA, MATE

O CTOBER. THE DAY BEFORE the annual harvest party at the winery I call Jesse and say, Okay, I totally owe you for all these conversations and all your time, and as payment I am giving you a choice of three Australian pinot noirs I just got in the mail from friends in the Lucky Country. You pick the one you want and we will open it over lunch at the bistro when your man Jason is making those unbelievable oyster fritters again, which he ceased to do for a while, which bummed me out, the nerve of the guy to take my favorite thing off the menu, what was he thinking?

Okay, says Jesse. What are my options?

Yering Station 2001, from the Yarra Valley, the first vineyard in Victoria, founded 1838. Or another Yarra Valley, Healesville 2002, made from the Mariafeld clone of the poet's grape. Or a Stonier 2003 from the Mornington Peninsula south of Melbourne; that's a wine I had on the quay in Sydney with two Australian friends, terrific wine.

I'll take the Mariafeld, says Jesse. Be interesting to taste a clone we don't use.

Done, I say. Sometime this winter, when things are slow in the winery, and this book is all locked up at the press and I can't screw it up anymore, and it's been raining and raining, we will sit us down by the fire in the bistro and split a bottle of sunlight from the Yarra Valley.

Good on ya, mate, says Jesse, and he hangs up laughing but I spent much of the rest of the day mentally along the Yarra River in Australia, remembering the day I was there with a friend and his son, the boy puttering along the riverbank skipping rocks and watching for turtles in the way of all small boys by all rivers, and that makes me remember a pub near the

Yarra where one night I was sipping a glass of pinot noir and
two real live professional philosophers sat down next to me and
we got into a great wild conversation about how thoughts are
actual electrical explosions in the wet living mud of the brain,
and how genetics is actually a form of mathematics if you think
about it, and this in turn made me remember a conversation I
had with a college student on Flinders Lane on the banks of the
Yarra and she said, The fact is that nations are best formed by
rebellion against the mother empire, and while America fought
off the iron grip of the mother, Australia did not, although, as
she added, We fought for our life as a nation for the first time
only in 1942 against the Japanese, and those battles up on New
Guinea were really the birth throes of my country, and that
conversation reminded me finally of talking one morning near
the Yarra with the Australian visionary Martin Flanagan, who
told me his hope for his country was that the dense ancient
magic river of aboriginal culture there for sixty thousand years
would entwine and braid with the dense ancient magical river
of Gaelic culture that poured across the sea from Ireland and
Scotland courtesy of the former British empire, and from the
marriage of these two cultures so muscled with saga and song
and magic and poetry and endurance might come a wholly new
nation, one unlike any that had ever been in the world before,
one that was neither black nor white but the color of hope and
mercy, one in which true stories and not deft lies were the
political and spiritual compasses, one that might be a lodestar
for the world to come, a world in which race and religion and
tribe stopped being the bloody fences they've always been and
became roots from which might grow the most amazing new
forms of us, and that, said Martin, smiling in the green riot of
his garden, that would be something for which to open the best
bottle in the house, eh?

    That night I open the other Yarra Valley pinot noir and
sip it slowly and pray.

93E! 98YH 01TH 92R(FH)!

O CTOBER. A FEW DAYS after the harvest party I wander
up to the winery and find Jesse fixing something
behind the row of steel tanks. Okay, I say to Jesse, as he
checks a spigot or hose or something behind one of the vast
steel tanks, Okay, here's a question: what's the best Lange
pinot noir *ever*? and to my utter surprise his voice answers
immediately, without the slightest hesitation, with none of
his usual smiling caution,

The 93 estate pinot noir.

What?

Unbe*liev*able grapes that
year, he says, his voice echoing
weirdly.

I am so startled by his
bluntness that I am
stumbletongued for a moment
and I stall for time by asking
questions.

Uh, all-time top three? I
say to the tank.

93 estate pinot noir, he
says promptly, and the 98
Yamhill Vineyards pinot noir,
which is Wally's vineyard, and
then probably the 01 Three
Hills, or the 92 reserve pinot
noir, which that year was half
grapes from Freedom Hill, you
know, that's Dan's vineyard
down by Salem.

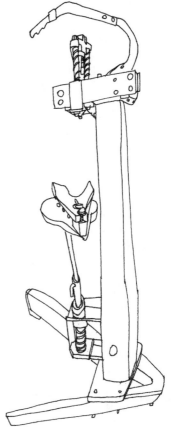

Uh, yeh, I say, scribbling down the years so my notes look like a football play or a locker combination: 93E! 98YH 01TH 92R(FH)!

You writing this down? asks the tank.

Yeh.

Don't bother. The 02s will be better.

Really? The best wines in seventeen years?

Trust me.

Why?

Ter*rif*ic grapes.

Talented winemakers?

Perfect weather, he says, and I can *hear* him grinning behind the tank.

SOIL UNDER SOLE

O CTOBER. I DRIVE TO Dundee through a dense fog but
then as I drive up the hill to the winery I drive right up
out of the fog into a glorious glittering gleaming day, the fog
and mist swirling and whirling and tendrilling below like a
cottony sea, and something about the way the day above the
valley is a special secret gift to anyone up on the hills makes for
a sort of unspoken giddiness in the air, a willingness to lay
aside the things you were supposed to do and just eat the
incredible gift of light with your eager thirsty skin, which
giddiness I feel my own personal solipsistic self, and I put aside
the careful accounting of shipping and distribution patterns
and records I had planned for the afternoon and get a glass of
pinot noir from Gabe and go sit on the warm grass in the
glorious light and let the sun soak into me like crisp golden
water, and I find myself thinking, not for the first time, that a
brilliant day in October in Oregon is maybe the best day
anytime anywhere anyhow, what with the clarity of the light,
and the certain knowledge that soon the light will be gone
again and the world will be moist mist for months, and it turns
out that Don and Jesse apparently feel the same odd giddiness
today, because for once they too get glasses of wine and come
and sit on the lawn, and we get to talking about the land under
the lawn, and how there are few if any lots of good pinot noir
land left in the Red Hills, and I tell them of three recent
conversations I have had with other winemakers in the Hills
who said bluntly and honestly that yes, there was lots of
vineyardable land available in Oregon, maybe as much as a
hundred thousand acres, and maybe thirty or forty thousand
acres in the northern Willamette Valley, and even some acres
available in the coveted famed legendary Red Hills, though the

available land left in the hills was not very good for growing pinot, and I tease Don and Jesse about how many times they have said to me adamantly that they were done buying land, there was no way they could expand without turning into another whole kind of company which they didn't want to do, and Don and Jesse look at each other and grin.

Whaaat? I ask.

Well, says Don, we just bought fifteen more acres.

Say what?

Wendy bought fifteen acres on Tuesday, says Jesse.

No way.

Way.

What, someone else's vineyard?

No no, says Don cheerfully, we finally bought the neighbors' land.

And he explains that he and Wendy and Jesse have for years wanted to buy the adjoining fields and meadows, the ones filled with grasses way taller than me and ground squirrels like nervous fur hats and goldfinches riding bucking thistles like feathered cowboys on flowery broncos, but the neighbors had never put it up for sale, and the Langes and the neighbors never entered into any formal agreement about if and when the land ever came up for sale, because that wasn't the way they related to each other on the hill, everyone has different ways of relating to their neighbors, as Jesse says carefully, but Don had said to them, well, if ever, and finally If Ever arrived and the neighbors decided to sell, and the only people they would ever sell it to of course were the Langes, seeing as that's how they related to each other up there on Buena Vista Road, so Wendy closed the deal Tuesday, and now, says Don, twirling his glass, we have fifteen more acres than we did a week ago. Which is an exciting and scary thought.

Are you going to plant right away?

Oh, sure, says Don. You want to get your vines in as quick as you can, probably February.

What're you going to plant? All pinot noir?

Well, I have ideas about that, and my young winemaking partner here has ideas about that, and we are in a period of discussion and negotiation about that, says Don, grinning. Suffice it to say that we will be planting some combination of pinot noir and chardonnay. Riesling is under discussion. Pinot blanc, no.

What about the grapes you were dreaming of, like tempranillo?

My winemaking partner, says Don, has convinced me that these hills were put here for one primary reason, which is pinot noir, and one secondary reason, which is chardonnay, and he is a persuasive young man, and he is also the general manager of the corporation, and after five years of making wine in these hills he's pretty knowledgeable about wine in these hills, so my feeling is that the executive winemaker will heed the young man's advice and an amicable agreement will be brokered. But we will have more discussion and negotiation about it. The executive winemaker, he concludes, is a stubborn man hard to talk to sometimes. So I hear.

Wow, I say, fifteen more acres. I can't believe it.

Believe it, says Jesse. And all the credit goes to Wendy. You wouldn't believe all the stuff she does quietly behind the scenes but if that stuff doesn't get done we go out of business right quick. Payroll, taxes, health care, all compliance for state and federal stuff and for shipping and distribution and bonding details, licensing and everything, printing, real estate matters, which are sort of crucial to the corporation. She works *hard*.

I'll say, says Don.

Plus she's executive director of goats, I say.

Don't bring them into the conversation, says Don. I'm having a lovely day and I don't want to think about the goats.

THE WORKHORSE

NOVEMBER. I WANDER UP to the winery and account the wines. The Langes annually make and sell thirteen wines, ranging in price from a $12 pinot gris to a $50 pinot noir. In fact they make four $50 pinot noirs, each from a single hillside vineyard in the valley: their own, one to the southwest, one to the northwest, and the one high on the west wall of the valley—the vineyard that produces the wine that tastes like clove, oranges, cocoa, sage, plums, cherries, and a grain of allspice in the nose.

They also make a riesling, a pinot blanc, two chardonnays (one a "reserve," made from the grapes Don considers the pick of the litter), a reserve pinot gris, and three pinot noirs made of blended wines. One of these is my favorite Lange wine, the Three Hills Cuvee, which is made of wine from three of their four hillside vineyards; this is a sturdy sinuous complicated wine, something to have two or three times a year in moments of celebration or seduction or complete financial abandon, for it costs thirty-eight dollars a bottle, which is a remarkable lot of money for something that will be gone in an hour leaving only happy memories and empty glasses and perhaps a bra on the lampshade.

But the Three Hills Cuvee, much as it has occasionally enlivened my evenings, is not the most intriguing of Lange's wines. To me the most interesting of all is the eighteen-dollar Willamette Valley Pinot Noir—the workhorse of the winery, the foot soldier, the flag-bearer. It's the one that sells the most, the one they make the most, the one that generally is the general public's introduction to Lange Winery. It's a paradox of a pinot: It's the cheapest but it is not cheap. It is the least renowned but it reflects the most craft. It draws the least applause but should arguably draw the most.

It's really where you see my dad at the top of his game, says Jesse. I mean, it's easy, in a way, to make a great wine from a single vineyard, if you get great fruit, and handle it right, and know what you're doing. And the single vineyard wines are sexy, they sell for the most money, wine geeks prize them, and they are wonderful examples of terroir, the flavor of a particular place. But blending fruit from different vineyards to make a wine consistent in style from year to year, that's not easy. Blending wines from different vineyards to make a wine greater than the sum of its parts, that's not easy either. That takes feel and skill. That's where my dad is a great winemaker. He has to smell and feel and taste the grapes, and guess at what kind of wine they'll make, and then taste them in barrel again and again, and mix and match them, and all this while also blending the other two pinot noirs, and blending all six of the whites, which is a lot of wine to keep in his head, but the fact is that every year the Willamette Valley pinot noir has a certain taste and feel that marks it as ours. Which is pretty cool.

We talk about the price of the workhorse, and I note that while eighteen bucks is by no means cheap, not in a world where you can buy an almost drinkable red wine from Monsieur Charles Shaw for two bucks, a mere eighteen bucks for a pinot noir from the Red Hills of Dundee, made by the Langes père and fils, seems like a bargain, in a sense, considering that comparable pinot noir blends from the area sell for upwards of forty or fifty dollars a bottle. So why is Lange Winery's foundational wine not sold for upwards of forty or fifty dollars a bottle?

Because we want to make and sell a pinot noir that most people can afford at least once in while, says Jesse. Because we would rather have a lot of people drinking a little Lange than a

few people drinking a lot of Lange. Because we take a certain pride in having a really good pinot noir that even people like you can buy sometimes. That matters a lot to my dad and I find that it matters to me. It's hard to explain. There's a lot in the wine business that's hard to explain in the end. I mean, it's farming, you know? It's hard work, and a lot of money borrowed to get into the business, and you're completely helplessly dependent on the weather, and you have to market yourself hard every day of the year, but there's something about making wine and people enjoying your wine that's just . . . hard to explain. Which is, come to think of it, why you're here, isn't it? To try to explain it?

Yup, I say, and I drive home thinking about how many things matter more to us than we can ever adequately explain.

THE GRAIL

December. My wife and I wander up to the vineyard to taste through barrels with Jesse so as to taste the whole spectrum from raw shaggy pinot noir just barreled after harvest in September all the way through to mature stunning pinot noir ready to be bottled in January or February, says Jesse, right before we have to plant the new acres, and mention of the new acres sets Don to talking about what he wants to plant there and when and how and why.

I figure ten acres of pinot noir and two of chardonnay, he says. That will give us twenty-seven acres all told, and we can plant another three acres here and there, so ultimately we'll have thirty acres under vine, which is about right. There's some unplantable land, see, right out here near the fir trees [we step out the door of the winery and a hawk the size of a tent flops away annoyed] and down in the corner [gesturing with the proud air of a laird] and the winery and the house unfortunately do take up some space [one of the dogs takes a long leisurely leak on a bush] and besides if we planted any more we'd have to be bigger which we're not.

I ponder the zen of this remark for a while unsuccessfully and then we get to talking about grapes that might or might not be good ideas here like nebbiolo, which I want him to try and he says no way, and tempranillo, which he wants to try and which I quietly suspect he will want to plant on the three unassigned acres, and this reminds me of the famous cabernet sauvignon misadventure and I ask him a question I have long wanted to ask: Is there any more Faux Pax in the world?

Hmm, he says. There might be some in the basement, and then he gets called away and I get called away, but a while

later when I wander back through the tasting room I see a
bottle of wine standing next to my notebook: Lange Winery
Faux Pax 1994, with a photograph of Archie the dog grinning
from the label.

There are three hundred barrels in the barrel room, each
of which contains enough wine for three hundred bottles, so
there is essentially a sea of terrific wine in the barrel room, so
I walk mighty carefully. The barrels are stacked three rows
high and the temperature is a steady 60 degrees all day and all
night and all year. Running along the floor down each of the
two long alleys is a grilled gutter. Jesse notes proudly that they
run a meticulously clean barrel room here, clean to the point
of neurosis, because careless and sloppy in this context can
easily spoil many thousands of dollars worth of fine wine, but
still, what with winemakers and employees and occasional
guests pouring out the dregs from their glasses, and what with
spillage from wine thieves when extracts are drawn from
barrels, and spillage when wine is transferred from cask to
cask, or pumped from tank to cask, or piped from barrels for
various and sundry reasons, or the occasional minor accident,
the fact is that a good deal of good wine has gone to ground
here, gone back to the soil from which it was born, over the
last ten years.

I stare at the gutters sadly.

Form of recycling really, says Jesse cheerfully.

Good point, I say, but I calculate that if a bottle of wine a
week has washed into the gutters over a decade then
something like five hundred bottles of excellent wine has
returned untouched and untasted into the very hill from
which it came, which is a metaphor for something or other.

I had asked Jesse if we could taste a range of pinot noir
from shaggy to superb, to try to taste the story as it grows
from raw to remarkable, but he's all excited by one particular

new chardonnay, and it's his winery, so he gets to call the shots, so we start with this new chardonnay, which was, nine weeks ago, grapes. Now it is a barrel of fresh new wine and Jesse takes a sip and smiles, and says hey dad, and Don ambles in and takes a sip, and they look at each other.

There's that minerality, says Jesse.

Stone and citrus, says Don. Great color.

Still a little green hint, says Jesse.

They each take another sip and I take a sip and my deft research assistant takes a sip. I watch Don and Jesse closely. They look at each other. Don looks serious but Jesse is grinning as widely as I have ever seen him grin.

We have sixty gallons of this still in the steel tank, says Don quietly.

Let's rack it into three barrels, says Jesse, and Don nods and ambles away again.

Uh . . . how good is this, exactly? I ask Jesse.

Good enough that we are going to bottle it as our first single-vineyard chardonnay ever, says Jesse, still beaming at his glass. Beautiful wine. Still young. Two more months in the barrel, I think, but there's a firm clean tone to it, lovely balance all through, a lively texture. These are terrific grapes. Freedom Hill. That's Dan and Hellen Dusschee, in the Coast Range hills. Hellen brings cookies for everyone at harvest when they deliver their grapes. Unbelievably great cookies. We've been buying their fruit for fifteen years. Unbelievable fruit. Man, this is excellent wine. Let's taste another new chardonnay. Okay. These are grapes from a vineyard two miles from here. Good grapes. Very good. But see how this wine is a little tighter, a little smokier? This will be, or should be, a very good chardonnay, but not quite good enough to be bottled alone like the first one. We'll blend this with our grapes and a few others. This is good enough for our reserve chardonnay, though. We'll see. It's early yet. They're such little babies at this stage, the white wines. It's hard to see what they'll be when they grow up. But you get hints. Okay, let's try a new pinot gris. This is fruit from Yamhill Vineyards, which is Wally and his brother Ralph, they've been growing grapes and flowers on their land for thirty years. Wonderful grapes. That land has been in their family for a hundred years. It's just over the hill a ways. Wally loves his flowers. He grows flowers seven feet tall there. That's good land. You should see his flowers.

Don wanders back into the barrel room and companionably sips the new pinot gris also and I ask him what exactly he is looking for in a wine so mewling new.

An impression, he says. A snapshot in time. A general assessment of what it really is against what we think it might become. You take snapshots in your mind all along the way from grape to barrel to bottle. We're essentially looking at how they are evolving. You have certain expectations or possibilities and you check on what's really happening in the barrel.

And every barrel is different, of course, says Jesse, and has its own subtle effect on the wine. See, now, here are three barrels made by the same cooper, in the same year, at the same cooperage, these are your Tonnellerie Radoux, Brian, and all three have 2003 reserve pinot noir in them, but see . . . [he thieves a wee dram from each and gives us all a taste] . . . see how each one is just a bit different from the other, that's because the oak for each barrel is from a different part of the same forest. So we have every barrel numbered and marked with the clone, vineyard, and harvest date of the wine in it, for when we are ready to blend.

How do you know when you are ready to blend when you are ready to blend? I ask, beginning to feel a tad blended my own personal self.

We make lots of test blends and then Jess and I taste and discuss them, says Don, wandering away again, And that's an interesting thing, says Jesse with a smile as his dad vanishes, There never was one day when suddenly I was the assistant winemaker. There never was a day when my dad said, Well, son, I'd like you to help me make the wine, or anything like that. It just sort of . . . happened.

No thlap of clunder or anything? I ask.

Uh, no, says Jesse. Now, here, taste this, this is pinot noir, clone 114, from the bottom of our hill, the younger part. This is new wine, just harvested in September. What do you taste?

It tastes . . . ashy and smoky, says my discerning wife.

That's right, very good, says Jesse. From this clone we have come to expect a wine with ash, stone, plum, tobacco. You can taste the malic acid in your mouth. It's young but promising. Another year in barrel, maybe longer. Okay, now let's taste this one. This is our pinot noir from further up the hill. This is Pommard clone, from rows 36 through 44, the heart of the old growth. Ah, now, taste that? Thicker, rounder, denser, deeper, more mature. This is also wine harvested in September but it's a different clone, and a different part of the hill, higher, from older vines, and you can taste the difference. This will be superb wine, I think. Okay, now let's taste the top of the hill, the first block of the old vines. These are the rows we walk through most of the time, Brian, rows 1 through 18, Wadenswil clone, also this September's harvest, ah, now, taste that, even when new this is my favorite of all, it shows its quality year after year, you can trust it to be fine . . .

And as Jesse and my wife twirl their glasses and talk over the nature and quality of this particular wine, and how long it will be in barrel, and whether or not some of it will be blended with other estate wine, I stand there thinking about all the hours I spent among those particular rows in the fat light of

high summer, listening to bees and wasps and swallows and
hawks, and keeping an eye peeled for moles and gophers, who
would be good roasted with a cabernet, and for vineyard rats,
who would be good grilled with an estate pinot noir, and for
other cool animals you hardly ever really see in life, like
grouse, and walking through the nodding vines with Jesse as
he explains about cutting their heads off, and pinching
clusters, and popping a grape here and there to taste it, and
showing me how the canes will be pruned, and how the canes
will be trained along the wires, and how the buds from this
year will be the canes of next year, and now I sip the wine
from those very rows, *my* rows, from the grapes that hung
above me this past summer as I sat summerstunned in the dirt
and the BirdGard machine shrieked in my ears and gave me
heart palpitations, and it seems to me the wine tastes
somehow like that wild light and that red dirt and those high
hawks, and I open my mouth to say this, to try to articulate
the sweet simple miracle of wine, that this swirling stuff
actually is this hill, that's incredible, that sunshine and dust
and wasps and basalt and the greatest floods in the history of
the world have somehow really and truly been caught and
crafted into the bright red music in my glass, but I have a little
trouble actually getting the words dressed and out the door,
and Jesse speaks first.

Okay, last taste, he says, dripping wine into our glasses.
This is the 2003 estate pinot noir, he says, same rows, same
clone, one year older, just about ready to bottle. Pretty much
perfect weather from bud to bucket. Great grapes. Decent
winemakers. And . . . *man*, what a wine!, he says, startled, and
I realize it's even better than he expected, and for once his
dignified caution falls away utterly, and he says something I
never expected him to say and will always remember him
saying, something so blunt and bold that I scribble it down

immediately in my rainsoaked winesoaked sunsoaked hawkhovered notebook:

You'd be hard-pressed to taste a pinot noir better than this, he says, quietly, staring at his glass. That's world-class wine. I've tasted the best wines in the world, but I don't know that there's a wine better than this. I'll step over the line today and there isn't a wine better than this, not in Burgundy or anywhere else. I'll step over the line and say we are there.

Hey, Jesse, the holy grail, I say.

Well, he says, smiling, recovering himself, at least in one barrel one year, and he and my wife ceremoniously dash the last of their wine into the gutter.

Not me, though: I savor it to the last lovely bright drop, because hey, life's short, and every once in a while something is the absolute best it could ever absolutely be, which hardly ever happens, and is, all things considered, pretty cool.

NOTES & STUFF

As you can easily imagine, I bow in gratitude to every single person I ever spoke to at Lange Winery, especially of course Don and Jesse Lange but also by golly Wendy Lange, Gabriel Quitsland, Chuy Chavez, and Wally Stein, all of whom were weirdly patient and cheerful in the face of blizzards of questions, and me following them like an eager puppy, and getting in their way, and stealing their valuable time, and etc.

And particular thanks to my riveting wife, who says what she thinks, is the greatest mother I ever saw, and is a stunning artist. Her name is Mary Miller Doyle, and she did the gentle drawings in these pages, and I recommend her startling artwork in toto.

Also thanks for good counsel and stories to my friend Doctor Susan Sokol Blosser, who runs her own capacious winery and vineyard in Dundee (where she makes *ex*cellent pinot noir and pinot gris). And thanks to Sari White at Archery Summit Winery in Dundee, and to Arron Bell at Domaine Drouhin Winery in Dundee, both of whom cheerfully poured me piles of pinot and let me pepper them with questions. And Tina and Dave Bergin at Tina's Restaurant in Dundee, where I recommend that you have the salmon spring rolls and the potato leek soup, and Jason Smith at the Dundee Bistro, where everyone says *hey Jesse* and where I recommend that you have the oyster fritters, and Nick's Italian Café in McMinnville, where owner Nick Peirano has cellared a thorough collection of pinot noirs from the hills around him, from A (Abacela, Adelsheim, Amity, and Archery Summit) to Y (Yamhill Valley Vineyards) and including of course a generous range of Lange wines. At Nick's you should get the rabbit (braised in Oregon pinot gris) and the minestrone soup, which is the best there is, period.

Particular special pointed thanks also to my friend Dave Hanson, editor and publisher of *Wamka* magazine in Sheridan, Oregon, who knows more about the northern Willamette Valley than anyone, and who is a most generous cheerful man, and who loaned me his copy of the very rare *Indian Journal of the Reverend R.W. Summers*, which was edited by the fascinating Father Martinus Cawley of the Abbey of Our Lady of Guadalupe in Lafayette, Oregon. Thanks too to Abbot Peter McCarthy who lent me an awful lot of his time and cheer. I bow in shared prayer, Peter.

Circles and circles, each more amazing than the last. We can but gape and savor.

Most of all winewise I thank my friend Gerald Asher who is a terrific writer and storyteller and all three of whose collections of essays are wonderful. His books are *On Wine, Vineyard Tales,* and *The Pleasures of Wine,* and all three are available through Chronicle Books. I assign them to you for riveting homework. Trust me.

Thanks too to Amy Torack of the University of California Press for lending me a prepublication copy of John Winthrop Haeger's massive & authoritative *North American Pinot Noir,* which is an eloquent doorstop of a thing. If you are really fascinated by the poet's grape and its story in North America, read John's book, which is comprehensive; and you might read *Wines of the Pacific Northwest,* by Lisa Shara Hall, which is a tad more scientific-minded. I am indebted bookishly also to Penny Durant at Red Ridge Farms in Dayton, Oregon, who lent me Paul Pintarich's *The Boys Up North,* a brief breezy casual account of the birth of Oregon's wine industry through Dick Erath's eyes, and Philip Wagner's great testy personable classic *A Wine-Grower's Guide,* which is a great thing to read if you are interested in how vines actually are grown. (Also the eyrie apartment at Red Ridge is the coolest most romantic place in the valley to stay if you want to taste your way through the Red Hills of Dundee.) I bow also to Penny's husband, the tart and funny Ken Durant, with whom every conversation is an education. Also Ken was one of the first to grow wine grapes in Oregon more than thirty years ago. I note with a grin that some of the best chardonnay grapes in Lange's excellent chardonnay are grown annually by Ken Durant in the Red Hills.

For tales and details on flora and fauna in the valley I have leaned heavily on three tomes in particular: the *Atlas of Oregon Wildlife* and the *Birds of Oregon,* both from Oregon

State University Press, and the priceless *Plants of the Pacific Northwest Coast*, from Lone Pine Publishing. This latter is an amazing book not only for the botany-curious but for history-curious and food-curious readers, because the ten authors spend gobs of time talking about how plants were used for millennia by the first peoples in the Northwest, whose clan names are music: Haisla and Hanaksiala, Kalapuya and Kwalhioqua, Taidnapam and Tillamook, Quieute and Quinalt, Lillooet and Lushootseed, Kwakwakawakw and Sacwepemc and Haqemeylem.

I continue bowing: to the wonderful novelist and essayist David James Duncan, with whom I have shared many a good bottle of wine and piercing conversation; to my friend the able songwriter and singer Robino Barteletti, with whom ditto; to my friend Marcelle Mogg of Melbourne, editor of the excellent *Eureka Street* magazine, who cheerfully aided and abetted my yen and yearn for Australian pinot noirs; to my friend the graceful writer Mark Tredinnick of Sydney, with whom I shared an Australian pinot noir on a velvet night on the harbor in Sydney, which gave that wine a particularly savory cast, as did the tales of our tablemate, the great writer David Malouf; to my friend Binyamin Birnbaum, who sent me his hilarious essay on Passover wine; to Bill and Kim Horton of Port City Pasta in Lake Oswego, Oregon, who have pressed many an excellent bottle into my greedy grip gratis; to Ed Paladino and Richard Elden of E & R Wine Shop in Portland where I have procured many an Oregon pinot noir and milked them for stories and facts and opinions and sips; and to my friend the noted paragraphist Joseph McAvoy, a brilliant and testy force of nature who owes me a pint of the best ale for some reason I don't remember but which is totally legitimate. All of those unique creatures endured snatches of this book being told to them raw and none of them screamed, much.

And thanks to Mary Braun and Tom Booth at Oregon State University Press, who did not choke and snort and howl and weep with laughter when I said, *hey, have I got a cool slim wild little book for you* . . .

Last, and least, I feel a certain grinning moral responsibility to the reader who has gotten all the way to the end of this thirsty book, so I say bluntly that my favorite Oregon pinot noirs are, in no order, Lange, Bergstrom, Christom, Archery Summit, Elk Cove, and Patricia Green, and my favorite California pinot noir is Cuvaison, and my favorite cabernet sauvignons are Trefethen (Napa Valley) and Owen-Sullivan (Walla Walla, Washington), and my favorite pinot gris are Lange and King Estate and Tyee and Sokol Blosser, and my favorite chardonnay is Giaconda from Australia, and . . . well, enough. As a wise young friend of mine in Dundee says, I like everybody.